Bike
nom
ics

BIKENOMICS

How Bicycling Can Save the Economy

Second Edition

Revised and expanded and with a new introduction by the author

Elly Blue

Microcosm Publishing
Portland, Oregon

BIKENOMICS
How Bicycling Can Save The Economy
Second Edition, Revised and Expanded

Cover and design by Joe Biel
Illustration on page 7 by Meggyn Pomerleau
Edited by Joe Biel and Tomy Huynh

Microcosm Publishing
2752 N Williams Ave.
Portland, OR 97227
www.microcosmpublishing.com
bikenomics.com

ISBN 978-1-62106-240-0
First edition: December, 2013
Second edition: September, 2016
Distributed by Legato / Perseus (US, World) and Turnaround (UK)
Printed on post-consumer paper in the USA

Also by Elly Blue from Microcosm Publishing:

Everyday Bicycling: Ride a Bike for Transportation (*Whatever Your Lifestyle*)
Our Bodies, Our Bikes (*with April Streeter*)

Library of Congress Cataloging-in-Publication Data
Names: Blue, Elly, author.
Title: Bikenomics : how bicycling can save the economy / Elly Blue.
Description: 2nd edition. | Portland, OR : Microcosm Publishing, 2016.
Identifiers: LCCN 2015048990 (print) | LCCN 2016004165 (ebook) | ISBN
   9781621062400 (paperback) | ISBN 9781621068167 (pdf) | ISBN
9781621069430
   (epub) | ISBN 9781621067474 (mobi) | ISBN 9781621069874 (paperback)
Subjects: LCSH: Cycling--Economic aspects--United States. |
   Transportation--United States. | BISAC: SOCIAL SCIENCE / Sociology /
   Urban. | POLITICAL SCIENCE / Public Policy / City Planning & Urban
   Development. | SPORTS & RECREATION / Cycling.
Classification: LCC GV1043.7 .B596 2016 (print) | LCC GV1043.7 (ebook) |
DDC 796.6--dc23
LC record available at https://lccn.loc.gov/2015048990

Contents

Introduction
To The Second
Edition

In 2013, while I was still writing the first edition of this book, I gave a talk in Cleveland, Ohio about the economic case for bicycling. The event was held at a large bike co-op, and the turnout included a diverse range of interests—local bicycle advocates, regular everyday riders, and representatives of various city governments and agencies in the region.

As I made my case, the city councilor from the nearby suburb of South Euclid became visibly agitated. This came to a head when I introduced the concept of "induced demand"—the idea that traffic is responsive to development patterns and available infrastructure, so that, for instance, adding more lanes to streets would invariably make traffic congestion worse rather than better. She could no longer remain silent.

"In the real world where I live," she interrupted, "when you build a grocery store, people want to drive there."

I flailed a little. People who already like bicycling are the ones who usually attend these kinds of speaking events. I'd fielded semi-hostile questions before, but I'd never dealt with outright denial of the facts. I tried to explain the concept again, adding some more detailed numbers and examples, but she wasn't having it.

I glanced desperately over at the head of the bicycle advocacy organization who was hosting the event. His expression was perfectly neutral. Suddenly, inspiration struck. I remembered a conversation he and I had had the day before, when he'd told me that the cause that brings Clevelanders together in a big way is their football rivalry with Pittsburgh.

"Pittsburgh is investing seriously in becoming a bicycle-friendly city," I blurted, without transition. "They just won a national award for it."[1]

She huffed unhappily. "So what do we need to do to make that happen here?"

I couldn't believe it. For years I'd been laboring over stating the economic case for bicycling, mulling over studies and statistics, and carefully framing the most factual, honest, and compelling arguments I could. But when it came down to it, all these facts and numbers literally had no bearing. Only football mattered.

It was a clarifying moment. If the clock hadn't been ticking on this book, I might have stopped working on it right then and there. In the end, though, it came out at the end of that year. A lot of people read it, and I've been getting a steady stream of mail about it since. One of the top pieces of feedback I get is from someone who says that while they personally agree with the arguments in the book, they feel I have made a grave error at its core. *Bikenomics* is "preaching to the choir," they say, when instead I ought to be spreading my good news about bicycle economics to people who don't yet know how awesome bikes actually are.

I decided not to include the incident in Cleveland in the first edition because it didn't seem to fit into the narrative, but I've come to realize that it's an essential point. While my minor verbal scuffle with the councilwoman wasn't exactly a paragon of diplomacy or listening, it contained a valuable and well-taken lesson. Bike advocates, like many people who are impassioned about their causes, are prone to seeing ourselves as knights in shining armor, riding in on two wheels to tell other people how they could have better and healthier lives, build nicer communities, and be better citizens of the planet—all just by riding bikes! The overwhelming economic case for doing so just feels like the icing on the cake. But this evangelical approach tends to fall flat. The problem: It's not on the agenda of most advocacy campaigns (or lay advocates arguing in bars) to consider the needs and priorities of communities that we don't personally relate to—especially when those priorities don't line up, and are sometimes in direct conflict, with our own.

Learning how to work with the elected, as well as other leaders, is one thing (and it's an important one). While many city leaders may remain unconvinced by *Bikenomics*, I've been hearing a steady stream of stories from regular people, citizen activists who have been able to use the book and the arguments in it as a lever for real change in their communities. But ultimately, these sorts of overarching arguments about public interest are unlikely to speak to the immediate priorities or concerns of our neighbors, families, friends, and strangers, who all also have a legitimate stake in the shape of our communities and the allocation of resources.

One thing I grappled with while originally writing this book is that there are really two economic cases for bicycling: Both are accurate, but the interests they promote are not always the same. The first case is the one for economic growth. Bicycling is a lever for the type of development that can turn around a city's economy, boost a business's growth, and attract young professionals to move from one city to another and work for the corporations that serve as a major part of a region's tax base. This is a model of economic development that has been of keen interest to many readers of *Bikenomics*, and several of the examples in the book, particularly those of Houston and Fort Worth, have influenced them most.

The second economic case is a more radical one. Simply being able to opt out of the cost of car ownership or reliance on largely dismantled transit systems is a tremendous thing. In that cost I include not just money, but time, health, stress, and community. That freedom, I and many others have found, opens up opportunities not just for a better individual life, but for people to work together to shift the similar burdens that encumber our larger civic systems. In this case, bicycling can strengthen and stabilize communities from within.

The first economic case goes down easily for many readers who count themselves in the bicycle advocacy choir. The second one is a tougher sell. In an economy focused on growth, a person's value is measured by how much, rather than how little they can spend. In this regard, only those already secure in their status can see bicycling as something to aspire to. For the rest, bicycling is a disempowering, even shameful, recourse. It's a sure means of attracting unwanted police attention or violence, incurring expensive medical bills from being involved with a crash, and creating the assumption of being unreliable, insolvent, or even criminal by potential employers or partners. In some circumstances, a bicycle might be seen, at best, as a way for someone to save enough money to buy a car and gain the level of social status that comes with it as well as the implications for every aspect of life. Much opposition to bicycle initiatives is driven by this perspective—and hardened when bicycle advocates and bike-mad city leaders dismiss it as unimportant.

●   ●   ●

In February of 2014, I was invited to speak about *Bikenomics* at the 3rd annual World Bicycle Forum in Brazil. The inaugural forum had been held in the southern city of Porto Alegre to mark the one year anniversary of what is known there as "the trampling of Critical Mass."

A video taken of the event shows a peaceful crowd of cyclists cruising down a narrow city street. Amid sporadic shouts of *mais amor*—the country's ubiquitous phrase that translates to "more love"—bells are ringing, people are smiling, and a little dog yips excitedly from a trailer towed by one of the cyclists. The first sign that something is amiss occurs when a man in an orange shirt riding in the center of the group suddenly dismounts his bike and lunges to one side. Then, even more suddenly, a black car shoots through the crowd. People fall or steer away in every direction. The car looms larger as it rushes towards the camera until it fills the entire frame, a riderless bicycle bucking upwards alongside it. The camera swivels and we see disappearing taillights and hear shouting.

The next few minutes of the video are scenes of shock. People pull out cell phones. Workers run out from a corner shop to help. A woman tucks her hair behind her ear, visibly composing herself. Another steps one way, then back the other way, a stricken look on her face. People pick themselves up off the ground while crowds gather around a few who do not. A shrill wail heralds the arrival of two ambulances, and several people are loaded into them.

The aftermath of the trampling was shocking in a new way. The driver faced no criminal consequences. An extremely wealthy man, he hired lawyers who argued that the cyclists had frightened and intimidated him, and that driving through the crowd at full speed was an act of self-defense.

Because of that incident, Brazil's nascent bicycle movement was galvanized. The World Bicycle Forum launched the next year, and organizations in cities around the country sprang up to lobby politicians for safer streets, bicycle laws, and infrastructure, and to come together to open up bicycle culture centers, build parks, and organize rides. The bicycle was becoming an increasingly important part of the conversation about the future of Brazil's cities. At the same time, adding fuel to the fire, a much larger social and economic protest movement was erupting around the country, successfully demanding cheaper and better public transportation service, among other things.

Learning about Brazil and its bicycle movement was like watching events unfold at home in a distorted mirror. In the U.S., we have the same social divisions, we have protest, and we have violence, but they are somehow deniable, erased from public knowledge as though by some giant sleight of hand. In Brazil, every city boasts a vast army of delivery cyclists—riding heavy-duty bikes and trikes laden with huge loads of boxes, massive bottles of water, and sometimes heavy furniture moving slowly down city streets. The complete disconnect between delivery cyclists and the country's emerging bicycle culture was one of many parallels I saw with the U.S., heightened by Brazil's vast class divide.[2] The organized, socially connected Brazilian bicycle advocacy movement, like that in the U.S., was primarily made up of the relatively well off. The people I met who lobbied for bicycle infrastructure, safety, and laws, participated in Critical Mass, and organized rides and cultural events all seemed to live in apartments in the city. By contrast, I was told, most of the delivery cyclists lived in distant neighborhoods in Brazilian cities' vast favelas, or slums; many have a bus commute of over an hour each way to reach their delivery job. The class divide was stark indeed. I was told of a trend in predatory lending—a poor person from the favelas could take out a massive, high-interest loan to purchase an imported luxury SUV, a new wardrobe of clothes, and membership at an exclusive social club; if the gamble paid off, they would make the connections that could make their massive jump in social and economic status stick. If not, their life would be over.

Back in the U.S., the cultural sea change of 2014 was unfolding. A young black man named Michael Brown was fatally shot by a white police officer in Ferguson, Missouri, a city just north of St. Louis. Protests swept the nation, intensifying as more police shootings came into the public eye. Protesters were portrayed in the media as violent rioters. Stilted debates faded in and out on several active transportation email listservs that I participated in. Should bicycle advocates do something? Is bicycling a social justice issue? Is there any connection between a recreational rider wearing a Lycra team kit being harassed by drivers and a young Black man shot by police for jaywalking?

Several vocal advocates thought not. Bicycling is just about bikes, they argued, and we should focus on promoting unity through this shared passion. Others objected strongly that their own and others' experience of public space, including the freedom to walk and bicycle, is affected on every level by police profiling and the racist history of the built environment around them—neighborhoods destroyed for freeways and replaced with housing projects. The economic burden of transportation has as much as or more to do with these societal factors than it does with whether a bike lane exists, or not, or in what form.

Witnessing these conversations is what it took for me to understand that a bike lane could be an economic lever, when used unwisely, to divide and weaken a community instead of connect and strengthen it.

The claim that "bicycling can save the economy" is absurd if the only kind of economy you can see or believe in is one of constant growth and massive investment. Bicycles simply don't register at that scale; even the bicycle industry—which is substantial—isn't swaying our GDP one way or another. The bicycle is most powerful at this level as a symbol. New, upscale apartments and condos in Portland often promote themselves using bicycle motifs (which is especially entertaining in one case where a bicycle logo appears on a sign directing drivers to the complex's cars-only parking lot). Craft brewpubs, expensive organic grocery stores, and third-wave coffeeshops spring up in clusters, and new bike lanes always seem to be associated with them, on streets which previously were home to convenience stores, neighborhood barbecue joints, and families of fifth-generation residents. In this case, bicycling is being treated not as a necessary and utilitarian part of a community's transportation system, but as a high-end lifestyle amenity. In these cases it fosters a form of economic growth that serves the public on paper, but is part of a package that displaces longtime residents by bringing in a new, wealthier population.

In the U.S. bicycle movement, it isn't typically the rapidly changing cities of Brazil that we get our inspiration from, but the smaller, longtime cycling cities of Europe. Copenhagen, Amsterdam, Utrecht—these have long been the guiding lights of our advocacy. In the golden era of bicycling in Portland, which peaked in 2008, our city's bicycle planners and engineers were taking personal vacations to hang out with their colleagues in the Netherlands, and when they returned home they applied what they had learned to our streets. Speakers from these cities were lionized when they came to town to tell us about how we were doing it wrong with our Critical Mass protests, our car culture, and even the types of bikes we chose to ride.

We learned many valuable lessons and put them to good use. But limits have become apparent on what we can do with the tools employed by small, not particularly class- or racially-diverse cities with strong, stable economies and a high quality of living. In fact, data had been showing for some time that these European cities were losing bicycle mode share, in part because they were grappling with some of the same issues the U.S. has always faced—an influx of new immigrants whose vision of upward mobility—and sense of safety in the streets—made car ownership desirable.

Still, I was surprised when a group of bicycle advocates in the Netherlands held a *Bikenomics*-themed symposium and invited me to present via video and answer questions on Twitter. What could we have to teach them? Perhaps something about dealing with a race and class divide, I asked. No, came the reply: "We still do have cultural differences with some of the poorer areas having much lower number of cyclists and especially people with other cultural backgrounds (especially non-western-world backgrounds) taking up cycling less then other groups, but these issues are much smaller and totally different from what is happening in the U.S. where small groups set a cycling culture that then needs to become inclusive without losing its identity."[3]

This seemed to be a fair assessment, though I couldn't help but think that it must be much easier for a privileged majority to impose its values without resulting in visible friction; the Dutch advocates, instead of having a very different problem than their U.S. counterpart, perhaps just had one that was much easier to ignore.

This left me at a loss as to what to talk about, so I asked the Dutch bicycle advocates attending the symposium about the top issues that they faced. A few days went by and these responses came in:

• Budgets (at times there is budget to do something but not enough to do it well)
• Cycling infrastructure is too cheap (sounds contradictory, but because it is this cheap it does not get the political attention it deserves)
• People protesting that space is taken away from cars
• There is a growing group of people that think bikes in public space are "ugly"
• A sense of urgency that is lacking at times
• There is a large number of stakeholders but sometimes no one is taking the lead

I couldn't help but laugh. Are the concerns of U.S. bicycle advocates identical because we've modeled our bicycle movement—the questions it asks and answers—so thoroughly after that of the Dutch? "Normalizing" cycling, with an implicit comparison to these European bike cities where it's no big deal to ride and pretty much everyone owns a bike, has long been a stated goal in the U.S. Along with that comes a culture of concern about presenting a united front and maintaining positive messaging—pro-bike and pro-safety, but never anti-car. By modeling ourselves on these mild-mannered places where cycling is already mainstream, have we succeeded instead in taking all the urgency and interest out of our own movement? Perhaps the real cost, for us and for them, is turning a blind eye to the violence that takes place in our streets, and the underlying concerns that divide who bikes from who doesn't. By failing to acknowledge tough core issues, we are compromising our ability to make a compelling and urgent call for social change.

So I tried to light a fire under the Dutch symposium attendees. "We idolize you," I told them. "We will do what we see you doing. So please do something bigger, bolder, brasher. Take a stand. Point out the real problems for what they are. Don't be afraid to address social justice issues or to take on car culture. Make big asks and settle for half, rather than asking for too little and settling for nothing."

There weren't very many questions. I asked if what I said was helpful. "Yes, very helpful," I was told. I wasn't sold on that answer.

So I'm bringing the same exhortation to you, readers of this second edition of *Bikenomics*. Please, as you read this, think about the numbers, but also think about the hard questions. Think about traffic violence. Think about generational poverty reinforced by concrete infrastructure. Remember the stakes, both for you and for whomever you end up arguing these points with later. Don't let yourself be hemmed in by a neatly packaged statistical argument. Find out what truly matters to you, to those around you, and to other stakeholders you don't yet know. Listen carefully. Ask for more than you want. Ask for too much. Don't get so hung up on normalcy and numbers that you forget about the deadly serious state of our streets, or about the finer things in life such as football and fun.

Introduction
Detroit Bike & Brunch

Kimike Clark bought her bicycle half an hour before her first bike ride on a Sunday morning in August 2012. "I had no idea what was in store," she wrote later. "All I knew was it seemed like fun." After listening to the pre-ride reminders about safe bicycling and road etiquette basics, she and the group took off—all 17 adults and two babies.

"At about mile two, I thought for sure I would die," Clark wrote. She fell to the back of the group and kept dropping farther and farther behind. She wondered if she'd made a mistake. She decided to turn back. That was when she heard the soothing voice of K'loni Thorpe, the group's cofounder, in her ear saying, "Take your time." As Clark forged on, the group stuck with her, and there was always another rider at her side with encouraging words.

Six miles from their starting point, they arrived at the brunch restaurant. "I got off my bike and before long the other riders began to congratulate me with hugs and cheering, 'You made it!!' That was the moment I knew my life would forever be changed."[4]

This was no ordinary bicycle-club ride, and this was no ordinary group of cyclists. After having lived without owning cars since 2008, Thorpe, an engagement specialist at a health care company, and artist Zoonine Bey launched Detroit Bike & Brunch in 2012 as a way to meet likeminded people who loved Detroit and wanted to see it fulfill its potential. Every Sunday, between ten and twenty riders set off from central Detroit on a bike tour of part of the city, followed by brunch.

It's a simple and fun concept with a powerful mission. The idea was never to bike for the sake of bicycling. The group's leaders regard bicycling as a means to see their city in a new way while improving its health—and not just its physical health. Their manifesto reads: *"Through biking we're creating healthier Detroiters. Through our Sunday trips we support local businesses and help to stimulate Detroit's economy. By traveling more with bikes, and less with exhaust emitting vehicles, we are fostering a greener environment. And by doing all this together, we are strengthening our community."*

Living without a car was a revelation for the group's marketing director, Brandi Keeler, whose day job at the time was at an ad agency. "I see more," she wrote, "I meet more people. I've never been in better shape or felt more liberated in my life." Keeler totaled her car in 2011, and while in a panic, she suddenly realized, as she put it, "Woman, you have a bike!" With the money she has saved by not driving, she could buy all the organic food she wants—a trade-off she's thrilled with.

In the spring of 2013, I was on a tour called Dinner & Bikes. I met Thorpe and Keeler at my Detroit event, and we all laughed at the convergence we had separately discovered—that the combination of food, bicycling, and building community really spoke to people.

It was the third year Dinner & Bikes had embarked on this month-long tour. Local bicycle groups hosted these events, and that year, the program consisted of a vegan meal, a movie about bicycle activism, and a talk by me about the ideas that eventually became this book. All good things. But the event was less than a week in and I was tired, behind on a dozen projects, and already longing to go home.

The Detroit Bike & Brunch delegation radiated positivity, openness, and determination. Meeting them, I knew I had to step up my game. What's the good of trying to change the world if you're too grumpy to enjoy the small pleasures of a meal, a bike ride, and a good conversation along the way?

I asked Keeler if she could measure her group's economic impact. There are the brunches themselves, she said—the group can fill half of a restaurant and drop over $225 before tip, adding up to a good morning in Detroit's sleepy service sector. Even more valuably, they spread the word about the restaurants they visit through their robust social-media presence in ways that are beyond the ability of most of the businesses themselves. Two restaurants in particular have developed a regular following among Bike & Brunch members who discovered them on rides and brought their friends and family back later.

The group is growing and changing. In the first year, most of the riders were twentysomething African Americans; when I met them in 2013, it was beginning to diversify in age and ethnicity. They welcome anyone who wants to join, regardless of gender, religion, race, ethnicity, sexuality, socioeconomic status, dietary needs, health levels, or physical abilities, Keeler told me. The group's only rule, besides safe and legal bicycling, is stated on its website: "NO NEGATIVITY WHATSOEVER."

The regular riders' abilities are changing quickly. Clark, for example, stuck with the group after her first six-mile victory. "Since becoming a DBB member I can proudly say I have been able to ride up to 30 miles in one trip," she wrote. "Cycling isn't just a hobby anymore; it's a way of life."

And she isn't the only one. Keeler told me in an email, "In a very short period of time I've seen this group transform inexperienced riders into avid cyclists. I've seen diehard carnivores change their dietary habits. I've seen the group elevate restaurant perceptions for skeptical vegans and vegetarians by highlighting its healthy food options. I've seen grown women cry tears of joy after overcoming their self-doubt by trekking through a difficult Sunday ride. I like to think that these small changes, when compiled together, can create major cultural shifts in Detroit."

As these Detroiters and many other people throughout the US are discovering, bicycling is good for a lot of things. A bike ride is a way to tackle, head on, the biggest problems in our personal lives, our communities, and the world. There are real barriers to bicycling in most parts of the country, which include dangerous streets, long distances, weather, hills, and cultural norms. But as groups such as Detroit Bike & Brunch demonstrate, these barriers can all be joyfully overcome with a little knowledge, positivity, camaraderie, and community support.

So why are more Americans not taking up bicycling? The answer, and the solution, is in our economy.

The Free
Rider Myth

1

"Bikes don't pay for the roads." You see it again and again. It appears on editorial pages, in blog comments, and shouted out of car windows, often accompanied by the accusation: "Freeloader!" or something ruder.

The bicycle-freeloader myth is a strong and pervasive economic belief. It's implied in rules that require cyclists to stay off certain roads, or ride in a manner that does not affect car traffic. And it's enforced through media headlines, police standards, and the behavior and discourse of cycling advocates and detractors alike.

But is it true?

When you take a trip on a bicycle, you don't pay for gas, and thus you pay no gas tax. You don't pay tolls because bicycles are generally not allowed on toll roads. You don't pay a license or registration fee, part of which goes toward paving, maintaining, and policing the roads you ride on. Most car insurance companies don't cover bicyclists, so often you don't pay for that either. And you don't pay for parking. No doubt this all seems terribly unfair to motorists.

Of course, though there are many people out there who solely get around car-free, chances are good that any given person out riding a bicycle on the road also owns a car, or rents one from time to time. When they do so, they pay all the same fees, fines, and taxes as everyday motorists do, and just as grudgingly.

But here's the thing: Cars don't pay for roads, either.

The idea that roads are funded by user fees paid by people who drive is one of the great myths that buttress our entire way of life. While the veneer on that myth has been crumbling for some time, we have only recently been forced to begin to look hard at it: The difference between riding a bicycle and driving a car is surprisingly vast[5], but not in the way most of us imagine.

What if I told you that by driving a car you become a freeloader and a drain on the economy—that people who bicycle instead are subsidizing a road system that they're largely not welcome on? In order to break even on the cost of roads and pay for every driver who uses them each year, we would need 54% of commuters using bicycles as their sole means of transportation.

It's not great news for most people. Driving is one of the most heavily subsidized things we do on a daily basis because driving a car is extremely expensive. If you live in the U.S., a car may be your best, or only, way to get to work and otherwise go about your life.

Cars pay for about half of the cost of our roads, all told. That's it. Half.

So where does the rest of the road funding come from for all that asphalt? We all pay it—whether or not we drive.

Most of what we pay for the roads is not paid directly, but through our taxes. Every time we pay sales taxes on purchases, property taxes on our homes (directly, or indirectly through our rent), or income taxes on what we earn, a portion of all of these taxes goes into a general fund that our transportation system has direct access to.

But the real costs of building roads end up being much higher than what the transportation budget can afford. Over the years, growing road costs have been (and continue to be) paid for with borrowed money, which means these loans must eventually be paid off with the money from our taxes. With interest, that can amount to two, three, or more times the original cost of the project! Worst of all, this funding gap increases every year. When the economy drags, we drive less. And as fuel and material costs rise, construction grows more expensive.

Roads are enormously expensive to build and maintain. If you look only at the highway system, the user fees paid by drivers come much closer to paying for them than half, though the system still operates at a loss. But if you look at local roads, on which most of our daily travel happens, the gap is even wider. The cost to maintain local roads is, on average, more than six cents per mile for each car each year. How much of this do drivers actually pay? Less than a penny.

So what does this mean for bicycling?

Generally, people don't have to pay to ride bicycles on the road, and bicycling costs almost nothing—less than 1% of money spent on transportation infrastructure in the U.S. goes to anything bike-related. Furthermore, bicycles don't contribute significantly to road-related expenses such as potholes, crashes, or congestion.

The thing is, people who ride bicycles also pay taxes, which mean they often pay more into the road system than they cost it. By one estimate, a car-free cyclist overpays by an average of $250 a year—a few dollars more than the amount an average driver underpays.[6] While cyclists represent all income levels more or less equally, the ones who ride for transportation alone and don't own cars are on the lower end of the income spectrum. For them, this situation epitomizes what's wrong with lopsided systems, regressive taxes, and programs, such as the lottery, by which the poor subsidize the better off.

Consider this: To pay for the cost of keeping one driver on the road, you need someone else who's not driving—that is, paying taxes but putting minimal wear and tear on the system. Unfortunately, two thirds of people in the U.S. drive, and most of the rest travel in cars and on buses as passengers. Despite a growing number of bicycles on the roads, there aren't nearly enough of them to balance out this equation. And even if motorists were to double the fees they pay, and those fees were indexed to inflation, it would still not be enough.

It's a recipe for debt, no doubt. Our road system is in bad shape, and we haven't been able to spend nearly enough on it in the last decade to keep it even in minimally good working order. And yet, there's a constant demand for more roads to be built so that more of us can drive farther and more often.

That's just the beginning of the story. Roads, which are economically unsustainable in their own right, result in towering externalities; their costs or benefits are indirectly attributed and paid for elsewhere. When you take these costs into account—from health to safety to local economies to global energy—by the most conservative estimate, the cost to keep each car on the road is 30 times the cost to keep each bicycle on the road.

Yet not a month goes by without some clever politician deciding that the best way out of our transportation-funding crisis is to license and register bicyclists. Every year, it's up to weary bicycle advocates to do the math once again to show everyone that there's no way for such a funding scheme to break even on its administrative costs, never mind the cost of accommodating a sudden increase in cars on the road and passengers on transit.

The humble bicycle, long a scapegoat, may yet prove our salvation from a transportation system running at a deficit. This is not so far-fetched as it might seem at first glance.

Take Copenhagen, where 40 years ago the incursion of cars and roads looked very similar to that in today's U.S. cities. But today, 84% of the city's residents regularly ride bicycles. Each mile traveled on a bike earns the city, by one analysis, 42 cents. That same mile driven in a car costs the city 20 cents.[7] However, bicycling rates there have begun to decline in recent years, and city leaders are scrambling to make bikeways more comfortable and convenient; they know they can't afford not to.

In the U.S., we can't afford not to either, but it's harder for us to see that— bicycling hasn't grown into normalcy in the same way it has in other places. But when you consider that almost 70% of our car trips are under two miles—

comparable to a 40-minute walk or a 12-minute bicycle ride—change seems more feasible. More than two thirds of people in the U.S. say they wish they bicycled more often, and an increasing number are doing so.[8] The barriers are real, but can be overcome cheaply and quickly. And the benefits multiply and spread into every aspect of our economy and our lives.

I started riding a bike at age 21 as a means of transportation around New Haven, where I lived at the time. It wasn't until I moved to the much more bike-friendly Portland, Oregon that I realized that places didn't have to be difficult or dangerous to bike in. A friendly city commissioner here, a comfortably wide bike path there, and a trickle of revenue—as well as a growing number of determined, organized, and everyday bicyclists—had put Portland on the map. And the benefits were plain for everyone to see. By 2007, the bicycling rate in Portland had skyrocketed and people were moving to the city in droves, able to afford our ever-increasing rents because they didn't need to own a car.

And Portland wasn't alone. Cities all over North America were suddenly fertile breeding grounds for bicycle movements, from the hills of Seattle and San Francisco to the winter-harsh cold streets of Minneapolis and Montreal to the hot, sprawling metropolises of Houston and Atlanta. Even Los Angeles, the ultimate city built for cars, began taking to bicycles like there's no tomorrow.

At the end of 2008, as the economy went on the skids, I began working as an editor at BikePortland, a local news and culture blog devoted to all things bicycle. There, I noticed that while the bicycle industry was certainly feeling the pain of the recession, it didn't seem to be at the same catastrophic level as most of the U.S.

Meanwhile, at around the same time, corrals for on-street bike parking were being built all over town, and the businesses they were in front of noticeably fared better than the ones where they weren't.

Two years later I started a regular column about bikes for the national environmental news blog Grist. Writing for the first time for an audience that was not already sold on bicycling, I noticed that in every debate about bicycling, the arguments against it were essentially economic. There were direct financial arguments like the popular myth that people who ride bicycles don't pay for the roads. There were class-based arguments: "Only poor people ride bikes" or "Cycling is a peccadillo of wealth." There were opportunity arguments: "Working families don't have the time or resources to get around by bicycle," "There isn't enough room on the roads," or "Bicycling is unsafe and causes congestion."

When I began to investigate these objections in light of the growing body of research available about cycling, it stopped me short. I realized I had always subconsciously seen my activism and passion for two-wheeled transportation as a fringe cause: as a way to learn skills that I could later apply to real issues once I'd grown up a bit more.

What I found instead was validation beyond what I'd ever imagined. Bicycling became the answer for many of the world's problems. Environmental destruction? Bikes can help stem the tide. Health crisis? Bikes all the way. Distracted driving and the epidemic level of traffic deaths and injuries? Absolutely, bikes. Mental health crisis, depression, and misery in general? Bikes. Social isolation and community disintegration? Bikes. Food crisis? Bikes can even help with that. Energy crisis? Bikes take it head-on, not just in replacing motorized trips, but in creating the conditions for more energy efficient places. Economic crisis? Now this is the place where bicycling takes home the biggest trophies.

Of course, all of the above issues—from energy to food to traffic safety— are inextricable from the economy. Economics is an inexact science, but it provides a way to compare costs and opportunities across very different phenomena in a more dispassionate and, perhaps, a more efficient way than if we considered other barometers. Most importantly, an economic perspective has a way of cutting through the messy rhetoric of our current social and political milieu. Earning, buying, spending, and paying taxes are things we can all relate to.

Economic calculation can also help us cut through ideological differences between the importance of individual behavior and choice versus changes imposed by governments and advocates. Follow the money and you can see more clearly how the interplay between decisions at all levels of society affects our choices, our values, our health, and our happiness.

We are only beginning to account, in numbers, for the sheer personal, social, and global costs of our transportation system. Each new study that comes in is bleaker than the last. We need a massive change of course even while we are already spiraling into debt. The whole country is holding its breath, waiting for someone to figure out a way forward.

Sometimes, simple solutions (ones we don't have to wait for someone else to get rolling) are the ones most worth pursuing.

Whose
Streets?

In our early twenties, my best friend Anna and I had trouble figuring out a number of things. One of these quandaries was especially perplexing: How did so many people manage to own cars?

We both had fulltime retail jobs and made a little more than minimum wage, which was around six dollars an hour in Connecticut at that time. When I got an office job that paid twice that, I felt wealthy, even though I worked fewer hours. At my new wage, I went out to eat and drink every day, bought clothes, had a savings account, could even go on vacations sometimes, and lend money to friends. I didn't have a plan or a clue, but I was having fun. I suppose I could have traded some of those pleasures for a car, but it never seemed necessary when I lived in downtown New Haven.

Anna lived in Willimantic, a smaller city in the rural northeast part of the state. While I could get anywhere I needed to on foot, by bus, or on my bicycle, she had to rely on rides or to borrow cars to visit her family in a nearby small town, escape to a larger city, or go anywhere apart from a few downtown stores such as the one where she worked. She didn't feel wealthy the way I did. And she needed a car bad.

We did the math together on the phone, with glum results—even investing in an affordable used car that her dad would fix up and maintain would be financially ruinous to Anna.

"You should just do it," I urged her. "People do it all the time, so it must work out." I assumed this was one of those secrets of adulthood that just hadn't been made clear to us yet. Wisely, she didn't take my advice. Instead, we both moved to Portland, Oregon.

When gas first hit $4 a gallon in 2008, I was deeply involved in bicycle activism in Portland. It was a heady time—that was the year of the bicycle boom, with people picking up bikes all over the country. Even after gas prices dropped, bicycle ridership stayed high.

But people were still buying cars and the bestseller on the market that year was not a small, fuel-efficient vehicle, but a full-sized pickup truck. That model cost an average of $30,000 at the time, though heavy discounts and incentives brought the sticker price down for many of the half million who sprang for it. Those trucks burned fuel fast, getting as few as 13 miles per gallon in the city.

That same year, the *New York Times* reporter David Leonhardt took a hard look at how much people were actually paying for those trucks.[9] He estimated that if gas stayed the same price over a period of five years—the average amount of time a new vehicle is driven by a single owner—that truck would end up costing a total of $70,000, which is more than twice its sticker price and more than one year of income for the average U.S. family at that time. (Incidentally, gas prices didn't remain the same price during that time, but other costs have gone up more than enough to make up for that.)

Meanwhile, a smaller car by the same manufacturer sold for about $15,000 and got 24 miles per gallon in the city. That car, Leonhardt calculated, would cost $40,000 in that five-year period. The difference in total cost between the pickup and the car is a significant amount of money—and twice the amount comparing sticker prices would lead you to predict. It's certainly enough to mean something to a household budget.

There's a lot you can do with $30,000. You could make a down payment on a house or pay down a chunk of your mortgage. You could have a fancy wedding, fund an entire four-year university education, or take a year off work to travel or raise a child. You could put a substantial amount away for retirement. Or, as many Americans chose to do that year, you could drive a larger car. (Of course, if you're able to get by without owning a car at all, or only having to rent one occasionally, the savings are far greater.)

But do consumers generally do this math? The popularity of gas-guzzling trucks in the midst of rising gas prices suggests we do not. Even in 2012, in the heart of the recession, those same trucks were still the top-selling vehicles in the U.S., with consumers buying 645,000 of them—an increase from the year before.

One of the best estimates of the real cost of driving is put out by the American Automobile Association (AAA) every year. These analyses are based on the market prices of what the actual costs are involved in owning and driving different types of vehicles.[10] In 2013, the AAA calculated the average cost of driving a sedan at $9,122 for the year. In 2015, that cost had been predicted to drop to $8,698, due to plummeting gas prices and improved finance rates.

Despite a significant reduction in the price of gas between 2013 and 2014, the actual amount of money spent on car transportation rose slightly to $9,073 for the year, according to the Bureau of Labor Statistics. To put that in perspective, that's over $1,200 more per year than an average household spends each year on food, more than twice what it spends on healthcare, and almost three times what it spends on rent.[11]

It's possible to spend so much more on a car. And many people do, whether they can afford to or not. It's also possible to be far thriftier, of course. Many people save lots of money by buying used cars, driving them very little, and cutting corners on insurance. Still, as Anna and I learned, even a few thousand dollars a year is substantial—especially when the annual income of someone working full time at the federal minimum wage is just over $15,000.

The AAA estimate includes a fairly comprehensive list of the basics: car payments, filling up the tank, routine maintenance, oil changes, new tires, insurance, registration, and depreciation (i.e. the amount lost as your car's resale value goes down over the years).

But as any car owner is all too aware, this is just the start. Cars are made of unexpected costs. The AAA accounts for basic maintenance but not for crashes, major-parts failures, or speeding tickets. Perhaps the biggest oversight is parking—the AAA's estimates don't account for this in any way, either through regular payments or tickets.

Parking, particularly in urban areas, is the big one. In New York City, a monthly pass in midtown can cost over $550 a month.[12] It's far from the most expensive city parking in the world—a month of garage space in London will cost you over $1,000, for instance—but it's the highest in the U.S. The national average for monthly parking nationwide is a more modest $165, but even that adds up. If the AAA included this cost in their estimate, it would add 15% a year to their average, bringing the cost of driving that sedan for a year to over $11,000.

When you look at what people actually spend, these estimates are fairly accurate. An average family of four pays over $10,000 a year in transportation expenses; smaller households tend to pay a bit less.

What also becomes clear is the toll that our cars take on our finances. In 2009, people at every income level spent more on transportation than they did on food.[13] Among households that made under $70,000, nearly 20% of their annual spending went to transportation (though, even with incentives that year to buy new cars, including the huge federal Cash for Clunkers[14] program, people were clearly economizing—far less was spent overall than in the year before). And the working poor seemed to have it the worst that year—65% drove a car to work and reported spending between 8% and 9% of their income on gas alone.[15]

For further perspective, the poverty line in the U.S. in 2011 was calculated at $10,830 for a single person a year; currently, it's around $11,770. This measure is based on the cost of food—a cost which has gone down over the last century even as other expenses, particularly transportation and housing, have gone up significantly. Still, artificially low as it may be, as of press time, 16% of the population lives in poverty.

Many people already don't drive. By some calculations, a full third of U.S. residents are too young, too old, medically unfit, legally barred from driving, or don't own a car for financial reasons or by choice. That said, more than 90% of households own at least one car; the ones who don't are primarily concentrated in large, East Coast cities.

Most of us pay far more for transportation than we can truly afford. And more and more of us are starting to realize it.

In 2005, I saw an ad for an event called Wheels to Wealth, put on by a Portland-based, libertarian think tank. I knew I had to go. The event was a morning-long conference on the topic of providing subsidized cars to low-income families. Car ownership was seen as a path to employment, especially for low-income single mothers, and as a viable alternative to subsidizing public transportation.

The libertarians/think tankers made some good points When you're poor, you're often geographically isolated and lack good access to jobs. Transit systems in many cities don't serve the needs of the working poor well, and most have cut back service even from where it was a decade ago. Low-income people often resort to predatory loans in order to get a car. And there's a real correlation between employment and car ownership. In many cases, it's the best of the bad options available.

However, my sympathy for the cause was dismantled piece by piece over the course of the morning. The speakers were relatively diverse in terms of race and gender, as was the audience, but it was clear that the lower and working classes were not represented in that room—and any anecdotes about the experiences of the poor were met with derisive chuckles. The opening speaker set the tone, railing against the bourgeois fantasy of liberal cities, and the environmentalists' war against the poor. Cars are really affordable, she added—it only costs $3,000 or so a year. The woman next to me leaned over and whispered that the AAA estimated the cost that year at twice as much.

The next speaker told the emotional story of a family that was able to go to the beach together for the first time thanks to a van purchased with a loan from her organization. A grad student then presented her research suggesting that car ownership could play a role in helping people climb out of unemployment (though this and all other factors were dwarfed, she pointed out, by the positive effect on employment of increasing literacy). A transit-agency representative who was there to discuss an existing rideshare program for the elderly—homebound in the city's suburbs and unincorporated areas—inadvertently became the star witness, touting huge costs and travel times. Another speaker, the head of a regional business alliance, bragged about his two-mile commute, which he undertook daily alone in his car, and quipped that his only problem with giving low-income people cars was that they were likely to "end up wrapped around my front bumper." Several people in the room laughed.

I told a friend about the event later and she was beside herself. She had raised three kids as a low-income, single parent. The reason it worked, she said, was because she lived in inner-city Portland and didn't have to own a car. This was back before Portland was a paragon of livability. Back then, you lived in the center of the city if you're broke; you lived in the suburbs if you're affluent. Living in the inner city gave her daughters access to the city's bus system, which they rode to school, and she didn't have to work all the time to pay for a car—or to spend her time driving them all over town.

What I learned at the Wheels to Wealth symposium was, in part, a wake-up call about the limited choices the suburban poor have—for many, a car is indeed the lesser of a collection of evils. The barriers those folks were talking about are all too real, now more than ever. The opportunity costs of *not* driving, particularly outside of cities, can be tremendous, and too many people are put in the bad position of having to decide which unreasonably high cost to incur based on its relative highness.

This, I was beginning to learn, was the real secret of adulthood that made car ownership possible for so many people—you make the best choices you can within the limits you have, and then you have to deal with the results.

The Wheels to Wealth event was a strange mirror reflection of another sort of wheels-to-work program I'd recently learned about: Community bicycle shops around the world have some variation of the earn-a-bike, or create-a-commuter, program. Participants are each given a bicycle, a lock, a set of lights, and a helmet. They learn to maintain their bikes and to ride them safely, and are given maps and route assistance to get to their workplaces or to navigate job searchs. These programs are popular to attend and inexpensive to run, and are often managed and staffed by people who have graduated from them. And even the organizations that obtain grants don't cost the public very much at all—nothing compared to the cost of cars.

It's a libertarian's dream, perhaps, as it would be, in the long run, the best way to address the transportation trap of poverty: options for living and livelihood that don't require the massive investment of a car.

In 2012, I started exchanging social-media messages with Sarah Noga. A quick look at her profile told me she was one of a small but growing trend of bicycle-parenting bloggers—though something about her story was different from most of the others. She didn't live in an urban area with a strong bike culture and other cycling families. The year before, she, her husband, and their two young children (with one more on the way) had moved from Alaska to the farming town of Arlington in rural Washington State.[16]

In Alaska, they had been a two-car family. Upon moving, they sold one of them, for both environmental and financial reasons. They immediately started saving the $621 they had been paying each month in fixed costs.

That May, Noga and her family were in a large department store and happened to turn down the bike aisle. "I looked at the members of my family, five strong," she wrote, "and then back at the bikes. There was a glimmer there, a playfulness waiting to be explored." Noga had bought a new tablet computer shortly after selling one of her cars, justifying her purchase with the money she'd saved. But while she stood there in the department store, she decided to return it. She wanted the bicycles more.

She bought them on the spot—two adult bicycles and two kid's bicycles, and a trailer for the toddler to hop into when her legs got tired. The total cost, including helmets for everyone, was $735.

They still had one car, an imported SUV, which they had bought new and were now driving less and less. Even so, Noga estimated that the vehicle cost them well over $12,000 that year. The family had begun bicycling so much that the SUV seemed like a waste. Noga eventually sold it with plans to replace it with a smaller, more fuel-efficient car—but she never got around to that step.

Car-free life wasn't easy at first, living in a rural area. At the time they sold the second car, Noga said, "The farthest I had ever ridden the bikes with the kids was four miles in town. That changed quickly, but it really took some time to build up the stamina to pull the trailer with more than 200 pounds of groceries and kids."

As one might expect, the costs associated with the bikes went beyond the sticker price. Maintenance wasn't much—they spent $30 that first year on spare inner tubes and a bottle of chain lube. One slightly larger investment that soon became necessary was outerwear to fend off the Pacific Northwest elements: raincoats and waterproof pants were $50 per person. The biggest expense of all came when their first trailer turned out to be a dud. They quickly learned that it wasn't waterproof, and when one of the plastic wheels developed a crack, Noga invested the amount of one of her former monthly car payments into a nicer one. She deemed it, "worth its weight in warm kids, which is better than gold."

Their one major unexpected expense was food. "We do eat a lot more when we bike," she said. "I usually treat my kids to Mexican vegan food when we make our big grocery trip by bike. The giant burritos may cost more than we would have burned in fuel, but I love eating a bunch of calories guilt-free . . . so count it a bargain." Compared with the $20,000 annual savings of no longer owning their two cars, it's a bargain indeed.

One of the biggest barriers to bicycling people report is simply access to a bicycle. Getting started biking can be overwhelming, and it does cost money, but it doesn't have to break the bank. A low-end but good quality commuter bicycle can be purchased for under $500 new, though $500 to $1,000 is a safe range to estimate. Used bicycles can cost considerably less, and if you live near a community bike shop, you can get a good quality bike for free, in exchange for labor and learning. Add-ons like child seats, panniers, and sturdy kickstands also run the gamut of pricing, from stupidly high to nearly free. Cheaper bikes are available at large department stores, but more expensive bikes from local bike shops last longer, so it's a trade off. Or you could scour the Internet, thrift stores, and yard sales for a much cheaper vintage bike. A tune up to scrape off the rust might cost $150—about the same as buying a new bike at a big-box store. Helmets, locks, and lights are another expense— you could spend up to $100 for these basics, though you could easily spend quite a bit less or more, if you were so inclined.

At the high end, a fancy European cargo bike might set you back as much as $4,000. And if your heart is set on an electric pedal assist, that could add another $2,000 to the cost. Six thousand dollars could buy you a used car of decent quality, which is the kind of vehicle that many of these bicycles are being bought to supplement or replace. This high-end sticker price is not the norm, but many families and small-business owners are finding that this sort of investment makes sense. So are the banks in West Coast cities that are starting to offer special financing packages for bicycles.

As with cars, of course, it's the annual cost that really matters. There's no standard yet for calculating this for bicycles, though one estimate puts bicycle operating costs at an average cost of $100 to $300 per year, if you annualize the cost of purchasing a bike and its maintenance.[17]

In terms of what people actually spend, nobody seems to be counting—at least not with the same rigor that other transportation investments are considered. At the low end, you can do all the maintenance yourself, with the help of a book or the Internet. You'd only need to buy a few new parts a year, plus a set of new tires every so often; it's possible to keep your bike in good running shape for well under $100 a year. If you let a bike shop take care of your maintenance, you might end up spending as much as $300 a year, or a bit more if you like to outfit your transportation bike with gadgets and gear. A 1997 survey of relatively well-off bike commuters found their average costs were $714 a year, including new bikes, maintenance, gear, and special bike clothes. Any way you play it, it's a screaming deal.

Bicycles gain or lose value, but the amounts at stake are considerably lower than with cars. Because bicycles are simpler machines, a good quality one can hold its value for decades, and it isn't uncommon to see them passed down from parent to adult child 40 years after the fact. Moreover, the used bike market is not predictable—it's common to get a deal on a good used bike and then resell it, five years later, for more than what you paid for it.

Children's bikes are universally produced cheaply, and, therefore, heavily subjected to depreciation in the U.S.—once their original owners have outgrown them, these bikes tend to be scrapped. A few sturdier ones are on the market here, and these, along with imports of better-made European models, hold their value extremely well. More expensive bicycles generally hold their value better by virtue of being rare or imported.

But are bicycles practical for transportation? Stories of bicycling families like Sarah Noga's are inspiring, and the math is compelling, but it's still hard for many to really imagine the logistics of the transition from a car to a bicycle.

I remember being surprised when I first found out I could carry a television on my bicycle. It wasn't a large TV, but it wasn't a tiny one either. My friend was moving and offered it to me. I carried it out to my bike, balanced it on the rear rack, and strapped it down tightly with a bungee cord. Would it stay there, or would it come crashing down, spilling shattered glass all over the road? I wasn't sure, but it seemed steady enough, so I set off for home. There was no disaster, and I barely noticed the extra weight and bulk on my bike. No problem, I thought.

My horizons opened.

Since then, I have carried any amount of unlikely cargo on my regular bicycle, which is equipped with nothing more than a rack. A couple of large panniers attached to the sides of the rack is all I've needed for most things: going to work, staffing events, camping trips, grocery shopping, dropping off boxes at the post office . . . If I can't fit everything inside them, I'll strap the remainder on top of the rack, or wear a backpack.

I've carried bulkier things too. There was another (larger) television that required two bungee cords. There was a large office chair—the swiveling kind with arms and a high back—that rested upside down on the rack. Once, I debated the best way to carry a full-length mirror, and ended up resting it horizontally across the rack, just like the bicycle repair stand I bought and rode home with a year later, which had an amazingly calming effect on traffic—nobody felt inclined to pass me too closely.

Over the years, I bought a trailer, and then a cargo bike, and then a trailer for the cargo bike—that's when things got really out of hand. I've moved a full-size bed and frame (with a friend riding on top of the bed), a drafting table, a sleeper sofa, my dog, another bicycle and its rider, a load of 12-foot-long 2x4s, and half a garden's worth of plants.

Car-sharing services are available in my neighborhood if I need them, but I never have. In the rare case that there's something I want that is too far away and bulky to make bicycling seem like a good option, I've often discovered that I really don't need that thing after all. And in truth, the biggest things that I've carried by bike would be tricky to fit in a car or even a small pickup truck—but they sit on the trailer just fine.

One of my favorite things about the bicycle movement in Portland is the tradition of helping people move. When someone moves, instead of renting a truck, they invite a bunch of friends and strangers to help them move by bike. A dozen or more people ride up at the appointed time with their biggest cargo panniers and trailers. It doesn't take long for everyone to load up with whatever they can carry, be it a single houseplant or the fridge. The group rides to the new house together in a celebratory procession, and members unload and socialize for hours—all in far less time, and with less effort, than it would take two or three people to make the same move by truck. The host provides coffee and snacks at the beginning, and pizza and beer at the end, and it doesn't feel like a stressful move—it's a big party, the modern equivalent of a barn raising.

One kind of cargo I've never carried is kids. But sitting on my front porch, overlooking a busy bike route near a couple of schools, I see people pedaling by with their children on board all day. Sometimes the kids are reading books, sometimes they're chatting with their parents, and sometimes they're quietly observing the cats, butterflies, and flowers that would be hard to see from a car. Bicycling with a child on board seems like the most normal thing of all—something one could be proud of.

Everyone who wants to, or who has the determination, social support, or infrastructure support, can ride a bicycle, as recent times are proving. But the stereotypes persist.

One common bias is that cyclists are all white men who are professionals with good jobs. They wear tight, technical, athletic outfits when they ride, and they're seen as arrogant hobbyists who think they own the road.

The second bias is that cycling is an act born of poverty. One common assumption is that cyclists are immigrant laborers who work odd hours. Another is that they are criminals who are consigned to a bike by a DUII offense they didn't have the resources to pay their way out of. They tend to ride miniature mountain bikes on the sidewalk, or weave along the margin of the road while facing traffic.

Although these characterizations are unfair, there's a glimmer of demographic truth behind each of them. They hark back to the bad old days not so long ago when you did have to be truly foolhardy or desperate to ride a bicycle in most American cities. Even today, cycling is not widely seen as aspirational, but rather the opposite—a mark of economic shame and a stopgap measure until the rider can afford the status afforded by car ownership.

Today, there's a huge cross section of people who ride. As the diversity of bicycling grows, so does the breadth of options and interests of riders. Yet there's still a widespread belief that cycling isn't for everyone, which is impossible to shake until you or someone you know gets on a bike and falls in love with it.

Part of the problem is representation—bicycle advocacy has until recently been a monoculture. It's a holdover from the time when few people biked, and those who lived in wealthy neighborhoods were more likely to ride for recreation, while those who lived in lower income places biked for transportation.[18] Many of today's bicycle advocacy and industry leaders have come out of the recreational and racing subcultures, and the history of change is so recent that its effects are just beginning to be seen.

One problem is collecting data about cycling. Most bike counts focus on daytime commuters. The census further narrows the field by only counting the "primary" commute vehicle. Bike counts often focus on bridges and arterials leading to the center city during commute hours. And bicycle advocacy efforts also overwhelmingly focus on daytime commuters.

A person who bikes from one suburb to another, works third shift, or drives to work but bikes everywhere else won't be counted. People who bike to the train station every morning, are out of work or between jobs, telecommutes, or whose primary duties are in unpaid labor—such as raising their children—are also not counted. Moreover, as of 2003, commute trips accounted for only 15% of all travel in the U.S.[19] The other 85% of travel isn't reflected in census data.

So when a city like Portland, Oregon is reported by the census to have only a 6% bicycling rate—and only a third of those cyclists are women and fewer than that are people of color—it needs to be taken with a grain of salt. The real amount of bicycle use is unknown, but we do know that in Portland in 2008, when our bike lanes were just beginning to feel crowded, 18% of residents told the city that they bike to work at least part of the time.[20] That rate was almost 30% in some neighborhoods when just counting trips to work.

Furthermore, the latent demand for cycling is so much higher. By one calculation, 60% of people are "interested but concerned" when it comes to bike transportation.[21] Another survey found that 70% of people in the U.S. wished they rode bicycles more often. And the League of American Bicyclists, the pre-eminent national bike advocacy organization, reports that 85% of people, regardless of race, have a positive view of cycling.[22]

There's an enormous, pent-up demand for bicycling. Our travel habits could conceivably shift overnight; nationwide, a quarter of all the trips we take are under a mile, while 40% are two miles or less.[23] Countries that have invested heavily in bicycling boast that 25% or more of residents' trips are made by bicycle. It's not farfetched to believe that bicycling could become the norm here as well—a mainstream form of transportation that we don't need to think twice, or to write books, about.

The Asphalt Bubble

3

My hometown of Hamden, Connecticut, a suburb just north of New Haven, is known in modern times for one reason only: as the home of the Ghost Parking Lot.[24]

Ghost Parking Lot consisted of a line of 15 cars buried under a thin layer of asphalt. It was either an eyesore or a work of art, depending on how you felt about it. Installed in 1978 (the year I was born), it occupied a small corner of the vast parking lot of a strip mall built on land where an apple orchard had once stood.

That installation was said to have been featured in over one hundred art books. I knew it better as the place where students from the high school next door went to smoke and practice skateboard tricks. There wasn't much for young people to do in Hamden. I too spent a lot of time hanging out in parking lots and dodging cars as I ran across the busy roads between them.

As a teenager, I had an awed revelation one day about the Ghost Parking Lot. It was a brilliant and cutting statement, I realized, about the failures of the suburban landscape. I wondered how it was allowed to be built: such a subversive expression of the ugliness and waste that nobody else seemed to see or be willing to admit.

Years later I discovered that its creator James Wines—artist, architect, sculptor, and environmentalist—was actually making that revelatory and wry critique with his contribution to that inhuman landscape. The work has been called one of the first examples of "site-specific" art, which relies on its surroundings for its meaning. Wines had intended, he said, that the asphalt would naturally be allowed to deteriorate until the cars were revealed again.

Knowing that, the demise of Ghost Parking Lot seems all the more terribly appropriate. Perhaps somewhat predictably, maintenance became a problem over the years. The strip mall's owners had dealt with the problem by pouring another, thicker layer of asphalt over the cars. By the time I was old enough to take notice, five cars had been removed, and the rest were square-ish blobs under a layer of pavement, with the cars' details no longer visible.

By 2003, Ghost Parking Lot had become so dilapidated that the plaza's owners estimated it would cost $120,000 to restore it and $10,000 a year to maintain it. Ultimately, the remaining asphalt was removed and the now-classic cars were hauled away.

Though there had been no car traffic to erode the pavement, a combination of weather, neglect, and time had taken its toll over 25 years. That did not stop the owners from blaming the skateboarders for the artwork's demise.

"It is questionable how much of the destruction wrought by automobiles on cities is really a response to transportation and traffic needs, and how much of it is owing to sheer disrespect for other city needs, uses, and functions." —Jane Jacobs[25]

Much is made of America's romance with the automobile. Cultural explanations tend to prevail: The car is a sign of social status, and an autonomous space in which an individual can be free and move freely through the world. There's something to it; cars are all tied up with our ideas of coming of age, adulthood, and success.

Culture is such a strong force that our ideas and feelings about how we get around often trump practical or financial considerations. The Wheels to Wealth event drove home this realization. "My wife isn't going to spend $50 to have her hair done and then take the *bus* home," sneered one speaker. Much like public transit, bicycling has long been associated with one of two things thanks to movie portrayals and popular imagination: immaturity or dorkiness (i.e. men living an extended childhood), and desperation (i.e. undocumented immigrants or those who are caught driving drunk). Either way, the stigma of not owning a car can have real consequences beyond your self-image, and adversely affect your employment and social opportunities.

But culture is fluid—everything that seems set in stone can change overnight. Asphalt, once it's been laid down, is less so. And as I had occasion to discover growing up in a suburb, asphalt is only as good as the car you have to drive on it. Many others had it far worse than I did, living in isolated residential neighborhoods where, without a car, there was literally nowhere to go.

Our supposed love affair with cars has for some years now been turning sour. If we ever could afford them, we can't any more. At the same time, now more than ever, we can't get anywhere without them.

It hasn't always been this way. But as inner cities come back to life, a house or apartment in the suburbs can often be much cheaper than similar options closer in. "Drive 'til you qualify," say the Realtors, and so we do. As a result, many low-income families in particular are moving out of the inner city and into dispersed suburban neighborhoods.

But there are hidden costs of living in suburban areas.

Three quarters of all neighborhoods in the U.S. boast affordable housing—that is, if you look only at rental costs and purchase prices.[26] Much of the nation's housing that fits this metric is getting farther away from major employers, shops, schools, and transit. A suburban house or rental may cost less on paper than one in a thriving urban neighborhood; but if you cannot live there without owning a car, then the expense of driving cannot be extricated from the cost of housing.

When you look at the cost of transportation and housing together, only 28% of the nation's neighborhoods can be said to be truly affordable. Rising costs in inner cities are pushing poverty out to the suburbs. At the same time, the cost of cars is pushing many who live in both city and suburbs to live beyond their means. This isn't just a pitfall for the impecunious; the average moderate-income household in the U.S.'s metro areas spends 60% of their total income on housing and transportation alone. Both costs continue to rise quickly, while incomes increase more slowly, or in all too many cases, become lower.[27]

For low-income households, the situation is worse. The working poor spend a greater percentage of their income on transportation and housing, even if they spend less in total dollars.[28] The high cost of being poor is especially high when it comes to car ownership. A used car can be quite cheap to purchase initially, but it's also likely to break down more often. Postponing repair of minor problems, such as a dent, can lead to more expensive problems such as rust. Car insurance costs more for people living in low-income neighborhoods. And the cost of gas is the same for everyone, but the farther you live from work, the grocery store, or other places you must regularly go, the more gas you have to buy.

Even for those who don't drive, the cost of cars is higher. Low-income neighborhoods are home to more car crashes—apparently a result of civic neglect rather than variations in individual behavior—and more air pollution, meaning expensive health care bills and less ability to work.

The strain is showing on all of us. It's no wonder that we're all driving less, but particularly young people—and not necessarily because they're discovering other ways to get around. Like I did as a teen, they are going out less. It's the surefire consequence of a terrible economy. Nearly all U.S. teens have access to the Internet and are socializing online as an alternative to driving to the mall or hanging out in a parking lot.[29]

Yet what happens when these car-free youth grow up? Owning a car remains the price of admission to an adult life with a job, kids, and responsibilities—even in a relatively human-scale suburban landscape like the one I grew up in. As a teen, the roads I had to travel on frustrated me as insurmountable barriers because I had to get around under my own power. When I got car rides, those same roads made trips to places absurdly fast and easy. Living in a suburban place, you invariably had to drive—no matter what the cost.

The American love affair with the automobile has an air of Stockholm syndrome about it. After all, why wouldn't we love the machine that gives us the freedom to travel? However, there's nothing essential about cars, or the American character, that makes this love so irreplaceable. It's more that we don't have a good range of choices, particularly the poorest among us. But that doesn't mean we can't do things differently.

●　　●　　●

"Houston is the sleeper—the next big bicycle city that nobody knows about yet," Tom McCasland told us. We were at a bike shop in Houston, and he was taking my partner and me on a tour of the city's new and future bicycle-path network.

I was skeptical. Houston is a quintessential Southern city, big and grey, built for cars, and sprawling out for dozens of miles in all directions. My initial impression was of potholes, unpredictable driving, and the chaotic geography of a city without zoning. In the few hours we'd been in the city, we'd spotted only a handful of hardy speedsters on bicycles.

But all of that was about to change, we were told. McCasland had recently, in his role as a nonprofit director, led a gargantuan effort to put together a $500 million plan to build a 300-mile network of off-street bike trails that will link up the entire city. The trail system has been in the city's plans for a century, but federal stimulus funding was the key to unlocking matching local funds and setting the process in motion.

He wasn't worried about local support—big oil was on board. So were the airlines that are headquartered in Houston. Those companies, not the traditional allies of bicycle advocates, are also the city's largest employers, and they were having trouble luring energetic, young new hires. One way to change that was to buy up the cheap right of way around the city's many bayous, and use it to transform an existing piecemeal trail system into a world-class bicycling network.

We saw a smaller scale success story at our first stop: the bike shop where we were borrowing rides for the day. When the shop opened seven years ago, the owner recounted, "People were like, 'You're geniuses!' And we were like,

'Well yeah, we know, but what are you talking about?'" They figured it out two years later, when a new section of the bayou trail network opened up a block from their door and business boomed.

We set off on a ride down that same paved trail. After passing uneventfully through a residential neighborhood for several blocks, our path ended in a sharp curb and a field of broken glass and gravel. The lot turned into a truck path, which ended at a decrepit railroad bridge. We took a sharp right down a single-track path along the edge of the bayou far below us. It's the site of the future trail "that will connect the two largest working-class neighborhoods in the city with downtown," as the bike shop owner had put it. "When that happens," he added, "biking in this city is going to blow up."

The next part of our route was a gap in the system that would soon be bypassed by a pedestrian bridge. We had the choice of taking surface streets instead or riding down along the bayou's edge. We chose the latter and ran with our bikes down a steep concrete incline, where we coasted serenely along a path by the water. After a while we scrambled up another steep embankment, lifted our bikes over a tall railing, and were back on city streets that seemed a world away—taking the lane on a five-lane arterial as honking cars passed us.

Funding for big projects is slow. But only one year later, those first pieces of Houston's new bike network fell into place, with the city council unanimously passing a funding match that would allow construction to begin on the first 150 miles of wide, well-marked bicycle paths built for transportation.

A glimpse into Houston's future can be found in the success of Minneapolis. What these two cities have had in common is land: affordable right of way for off-street paths within the city limits. Houston has its bayous and Minneapolis has an abandoned rail network. Both cities also have visionary advocates, business leaders, and city officials working hard to create an inner-city bikeway network.

Minneapolis's extensive paved off-road Greenway system connects the major areas of the city; people can reach most of their exact destinations on neighborhood streets and a slowly increasing network of bike lanes and crossings. Once most of the path system was built, and a few key on-street connections were made, Minneapolis went from barely registering on the radar of bike mavens to winning the #1 ranking in the country for bike friendliness.

The city sees bikeways as an investment, not an expense. And this philosophy is paying off. Minneapolis is home to several of the largest bicycle companies in the country. Its growing network of bikeways provides, year round, a healthy and affordable transportation option for people across social classes, attracting young workers and the companies that employ them, and keeping the lights on in local businesses—not least, the one bike shop that does brisk business with its front doors opening directly onto a section of the Greenway, without a car in sight.

But can cities like Minneapolis and Houston have it all? Where such bike paths are being built, there are material questions of what they are for: A transportation amenity for existing workers and residents? An attraction for tourists?

Or, increasingly, as was blatantly stated in the case of Houston, are they built as a lifestyle perk for potential new residents—wealthier and, often, whiter—who are being lured expressly to displace the current population?

Some further light is cast by a recent set of surveys; in one, white, relatively affluent Houstonians rated improved bicycle and walking access to parks as their top priority, whereas a follow-up survey that focused on black and latino residents found that improving amenities in existing parks was the overwhelming priority, while only two respondents out of hundreds prioritized improving park access. The researchers who conducted the follow-up study noted that no similar studies had been done in regard to parks where concerns of underserved communities were solicited.[30]

•   •   •

"Our problem was not, and is not, a lack of growth. Our problem is 60 years of unproductive growth—growth that has buried us in financial liabilities. The American pattern of development does not create real wealth. It creates the illusion of wealth. Today we are in the process of seeing that illusion destroyed, and with it the prosperity we have come to take for granted." —Charles Marohn, Strong Towns

Our overinvestment in roads and suburbs begins with, and in many ways still boils down to, freeways.

The federal government never intended to get involved with transportation. A hundred years ago, transportation funding was solely a local concern. Roads were mostly packed dirt and gravel. They became muddy and rutted in rainy weather, creating poor riding conditions for early cyclists (the earliest of whom did not have inflated tires to cushion the bumps). By the turn of the century, the bicycle lobby was powerful enough to demand paved roads between popular cycling destinations.[31] These roads turned out to be a boon for savvy players behind the rise of the automobile.

The Interstate Highway System was launched by President Eisenhower in 1956. It was intended as a way to quickly move troops and supplies to all potential fronts if the U.S. were invaded in a third World War. It was a visionary project, the largest the country had undertaken. The entire system was expected to cost $25 billion (over $70 billion in today's dollars) and take a decade to complete. The Highway Trust Fund was created to manage its creation.

Most states already had a gas tax, which, along with tolls and other fees, mostly sufficed to pay for their local motoring roads. The federal roads would be paid for through a new federal gas tax. At least, that was the plan.

The founders of the Interstate planned for the system to be self-funding, through user fees. More roads would mean more drivers traveling more miles—and this came true beyond their wildest imaginings. But they were wrong in predicting that the subsequent increases in gas tax revenue would be enough to fund the resulting expansion.

Sprawl, as we know it, would not be possible without the car. The automobile gained an irrevocable place on city streets just in time for the new prosperity that came after World War II. Cities at that time were often crowded and poor. Those who could afford it now began to move into the suburbs, thanks to the automobile. They could live in commuting distance from city office and industrial jobs, but live separate from the mayhem with their nuclear family in their own small estate.

Over the following decades, urban renewal and inner-city freeways gutted the inner cities, and these new suburbs seemed more and more attractive. And as more people wanted to buy houses, the investment of building new neighborhoods attracted developers.

In the last decade, new development rose to fever pitch, aided by heavy subsidies to builders and ill-considered bank loans to new homeowners who could in no way afford them. Ultimately, the housing bubble burst in 2008, and ushered in a recession. The banks had to be bailed out. Millions of homes, jobs, and livelihoods were lost. What remained, and what we still have and will have for decades to come, are the roads . . . and the debt.

The gas tax was always low enough to entice more people into cars and out onto the roads, or at least to prevent it from being a major barrier to driving. But it has never been anywhere near high enough to pay for those roads.[32] And it yields less and less funding. Thanks to the recent decline in driving, the popularity of more fuel-efficient cars, and inflation, gas tax revenues are getting lower every year, even though road costs are higher than ever.

When I speak in public, I ask audience members if they know how much it costs to build one mile of freeway. The most common guess is $1 million per mile, with some people guessing far less and others a little more. The cheapest example of freeway construction costs I've found is in rural Arkansas: $6.75 million per mile.[33]

On the other end of the spectrum, Boston has the most expensive urban freeway systems in the country. The city invested in the Big Dig project, burying its freeway system underground in the early 2000s. The final, eye-widening, jaw-dropping tally: $1 billion per mile.

A conservative calculation of the average cost of a mile of urban freeway is around $60 million. For perspective, this is about the same cost, as of 2008, as the value of the city of Portland's bicycle infrastructure that made it one of the most famous bicycle cities in the world, with a bicycle economy worth far more to the city than that amount every year.[34]

The myth that the gas tax covers all of these costs is still widespread. As it turns out, gas taxes have paid for about 70% of the construction and maintenance costs of the Interstate system to date, with that percentage going down with each passing year. Local roads fare worse when it comes to user funding. If you take the nation's road system as a whole, only 51% of its cost over the years has come from direct user fees.[35] As the gap between what is paid in and what has been spent continues to grow over the years, this contribution will continue to decline and the rate of subsidy will keep ballooning.[36, 37]

But how are we to pay for road maintenance? The original Interstate budget may have included eventual replacement; but nobody knew then how long a modern paved road would last. Moreover, nobody anticipated the kind of traffic the roads would eventually carry. We know now.

The lifespan of the original freeways built between Eisenhower's era and the 1980s has proven to be about 25 years. Good management and resurfacing with asphalt twice over the decades can double that life expectancy. After 50 years, that road needs to be rebuilt again from the ground up.[38]

In recent decades, as cars and trucks become heavier and more numerous, this life cycle has shortened. Paving and maintenance costs are also growing far faster than inflation. This is exacerbated by the rising cost of oil—a major ingredient of asphalt, as well as a necessity for producing, transporting, installing construction materials.

The Interstate system was built over the course of just a few decades, and it's growing old apace. Starting about 10 years ago, freeways and bridges started to age out en masse; we have a couple of interesting decades to come because we're running out of money now—and not just federal money, but local money for local roads. In truth, we never had the money to begin with.

As early as 2000, the amount of spending needed for basic, safe maintenance of our national freeways and bridges was 20% higher than the $30 billion that was actually spent that year. More recently, according to the American Society of Civil Engineers, we need to make $3.6 trillion in infrastructure investments by 2020 just to keep up with basic maintenance.[39]

But filling potholes just isn't sexy. The great spate of road building set off in the 1950s continues quickly, and new highway projects are still political gold.[40] Skill at leveraging federal money for road projects in one's district is a standard metric of Congressional electability. The short-term jobs created by the construction are badly needed (though the arithmetic of jobs created by new road building never includes the jobs displaced to make room for the projects). And at the end of the day, voters want more freeways—it is the only solution we know to the daily nightmare of traffic congestion we are stuck in.

That, and our transportation system is a near-monopoly, as a result of decades of investing in horizontal expansion of roads and the places that support and require them. And as with all monopolies, a few players profit greatly while consumers pay dearly.

The apparatus is in place, politically, financially, and in terms of companies and labor, to keep building more roads. The only thing lacking is the money.

The Highway Trust Fund, begun by Eisenhower to collect fuel taxes and spend them on highways, has already received tens of billions of dollars in transfusions from the general fund to keep it going. And yet it continues to experience funding woes.

Loans are where one of the biggest hidden expenses of road building comes into the picture. The massive loans that are taken out to fund part or all of large highway projects don't come free. The interest adds up over the decades, and frequently doubles or triples the original sticker price of the project as it was sold to the public.

We're caught up in a vicious cycle of debt. We borrow money to build a giant road project. That project attracts new development, which brings more traffic. Eventually the road needs to be expanded. Since the initial debt has not been fully paid off, a new, larger loan is taken out to fund the project and pay off the original one. The money is borrowed against the promise of further development to bring in new tax revenue. And so it continues.

Charles Marohn, an engineer and planner from rural Minnesota, as well as the author of the blog *Strong Towns*, writes compellingly that this is "like a classic Ponzi scheme, with ever-increasing rates of growth necessary to sustain long-term liabilities."

Marohn makes a persuasive case. "In sixty years of building endlessly outward," he writes, "we have reaped significant short term financial gains. But the cost is long-term financial obligations of a much greater magnitude. Every time the bill comes due, we have to double down."

"The public debt we have used to build a vast network of roads and utilities is unsustainable," he adds, "but this is nothing compared to the private debt that American households have taken on in the form of high interest mortgages and crippling transportation bills."

The short-term gains were bonanzas for many, and still are for a dwindling few. The long-term consequences are, as we are now discovering, devastating.

The personal costs of driving illustrate this predicament. One of the largest expenses included in the AAA's cost-of-driving analysis—an average of $3,500, which is more than a third of the total cost of car ownership in a year—is depreciation. When I first saw this, I didn't understand why it was included, and assumed that it was being used to inflate their estimates. But the more I learn, the more I realize that this is the most important line item on their list.

When you buy a new car and drive it off the lot, it begins to lose value. If you want to turn around and sell it the next day, you'll get back considerably less money than you just spent—maybe only half as much, depending on the vagaries of the used-car market. When we make other large investments, like houses or jewelry, we do so with the understanding that they will keep their value or even grow in value, providing us with stability and even wealth in the long run. When this doesn't happen, it can cause us to struggle financially. When it begins to systematically not happen, as was the case during the 2008 recession, it is a national crisis.

In this way, a car has never been a good investment. No matter how good the car is, how well you care for it, or how much utility and enjoyment you get from using it, you end up losing money in the long run.

Depreciation is, for many individual consumers, a hidden cost. But any responsible accounting of the costs of driving must include it. The fact that such a large and unprofitable investment is necessary for living and working in most areas of this country is a major source of poverty for many individuals, and it is a hidden source of inequality and loss of opportunity on a national scale.

The same exact principle is at work in our road system.

A freeway, once built, immediately begins to deteriorate and become congested. It replaces whatever revenue-generating land, property, or people that had previously been there. Once built, it loses its ability to provide the jobs and development opportunities that often are the argument for building it in the first place. This is depreciation at the societal level. It's irresponsible not to plan for it, but we do not.

Road projects are sold to politicians and the public based on their sticker price alone. Like car buyers, we don't go into these investments fully informed, and we reap the consequences—for instance, it's unwise for middle-income Americans to spring for the fully loaded trucks with four-wheel drive (even a smaller, more fuel efficient car would be a drain on their finances). To invest in a large new freeway when there is already no money available for filling potholes on the existing state highway comes with far deeper and further-reaching repercussions.

If the AAA were to add a new line item of the cost of driving to account for the taxes that we pay for roads, maintenance, and interest each year, we would understand our financial commitments more clearly.

Unlike transit, our road system works by requiring users to personally pay for their own vehicles. This is perhaps at the heart of the sense many people have that bicyclists don't pay their own way: The roads we all use are often the same, but the personal investment required to use them by bike is nearly nothing. This knowledge surely must feel deeply unfair.

And so it is. But that unfairness is not the doing of people riding bicycles. The trap of cars and roads is a strong one—and the consequences are not evenly distributed. When you ride a bicycle, you escape it. There are other prices you may pay—opportunities are lost as well as gained—but many find that the trade-offs are worth it, and as more people take to two wheels and our streets change to make room for them, the deal only gets better.

Just as roads and cars necessarily operate at a net negative, losing money for their entire lifespans, bicycling and bicycle infrastructure produces a net positive return. This goes beyond simple accounting. Many of the opportunities lost while sitting in a car are gained on a bike. Fitness, health, and pleasure are personal examples. On a societal level, we stand to gain no less than the prosperity of a community whose residents are not burdened by debt, the integrity and stability of our common resources, and our ability to participate in a thriving civil society.

Superhighway
to Health

4

Every year I spend a month in a car and I get sick. In 2013, it was the entire month of May. Four of us drove around the Northeast and Upper Midwest U.S. on our annual Dinner & Bikes tour. We hit 27 cities where we met and were inspired by hundreds of everyday bicycle riders, powerhouse activists, and kind souls. The only problem: All that driving made me literally ill.

Not just classically carsick—though it's true that if I try to do anything but stare out the window I quickly regret it. And not just sick in the epidemiological sense, though it's hard to imagine a whole tour without at least one head cold. It's worse than nausea or sneezing—all that time wedged into the back seat of a rental car makes me feel mightily unwell in the old brain (from moderate grouchiness to paralyzing anxiety, and, worst of them all, a general numb over-it-allness). At first, I thought it related to stage fright and lack of sleep. But after a while, I noticed that the symptoms escalated on days with long drives and disappeared entirely on days with only short hops. Sitting in the car was making me physically and mentally ill.

I'm no athlete, but I do ride my bike nearly every day. My trips are usually short, just a mile or four each way, usually to the grocery store or the bank or a meeting. Sometimes I carry heavy things or tackle major hills, but I prefer a conversational pace and my rides rarely feel like a workout. Despite this, I've always known vaguely that when I ride more, I feel better. My annual car trip verifies it.

When we think of health, we usually think of diseases. We work hard to address them through preventative measures like hygiene and vaccination, and we work hard to find cures and ways to ease the symptoms. And we've been effective. Those who have access to the right medicine no longer have to fear a whole host of deadly epidemic diseases, from malaria to typhoid to whooping cough.

Instead, we have a raging epidemic of chronic diseases. These are diseases that cannot be passed from person to person, but are related to lifestyle and environment. Cancer, heart disease, diabetes, depression, crippling anxiety, and general malaise are frighteningly widespread. They can be treated and sometimes overcome—at least their symptoms can be eased. But there is no shot in the arm that can protect an individual from any of these ills. Prevention of these chronic diseases must occur on a societal level—in the air, the water, our food supply chains, and the shape of our communities. Bicycle lanes and zoning practices are the antibiotics of the 21st century.

In Copenhagen, a network of 26 new superhighways are being built to connect the city and its suburbs, and to connect the suburbs with each other.

Bicycle superhighways, that is.[41]

The first of them, a 10-mile route opened in April 2013, was greeted with open arms and large amounts of jubilant pedal traffic. It's the hot new thing, and completion of the rest of the network is eagerly awaited.

In the U.S., off-road bike paths such as these are rare. When they exist, they're often narrow, and tend to be built in places where the land is available rather than where they'll be most useful for commuters. The Danish superhighways are built and maintained specifically to entice riders living within 14 miles of the city center to choose cycling for longer trips. The highways are well marked and signed. Intersections with roads have traffic lights, and are timed to bicycle speed so that someone pedaling along at a reasonable clip would rarely have to stop. Solar-powered lighting and bicycle air pumps at every mile marker are among the amenities the new paths offer.

Of course, these are more expensive than your average bike lane. The Copenhagen system costs about $1 million per mile. The expense is shared between the city and the suburban regions the network connects.

Cycling superhighways have long been a taken for granted as part of the landscape in the Netherlands. There, it is the policy to build expensive bikeway networks even in rural areas where they will never see much use.

Without them, people would have fewer choices, and need to either drive or take transit long distances, putting a much greater strain on public resources.[42] Even these fancy highways are so much cheaper, and produce greater benefits than the alternatives, that investment in even the least trafficked bike path is more than recouped within seven years. They are not seen as expensive investments; rather, it's widely acknowledged that it would be too expensive not to build them.

The financial benefits of bicycle infrastructure are many—decreased traffic congestion and pollution, relief for overcrowded trains, and simply more options for people living outside the city. The healthcare system is where the real benefits come in, though. Copenhagen's bike-path system is overseen by the same agency that runs public hospitals, and the new bicycle superhighways are considered to be very much a healthcare investment— when completed, they're expected to save $60 million a year in health costs.[43]

The Danish don't have to make any radical ideological leaps to convince each other of the benefits of bicycling. They know a successful public investment when they see one.

• • •

When I first moved to Portland, I biked around quite a bit in my own neighborhood. But for years, I wasn't really comfortable on the road. Going anywhere farther than a mile or two away meant taking the bus or catching a ride with a friend. When I did try to bike across town, I'd often find myself getting into navigational scrapes, coming to a busy intersection without a clear way across, or running up against a cemetery that went on for blocks.

This was a few years before the city put directional signs on all the bike routes and painted giant markings in the road to point out the best ways to go. Figuring it out for myself took a long time. My learning process accelerated when I discovered the city's bike map, and again when I started to ride with other people who'd been at it longer. Eventually, biking around the city became second nature. Before I knew it, car rides had become a rare anomaly and years had gone by since I'd been on a city bus.

Then I moved in with someone who had a car. It was the first car I had regular access to since my late teens, and the one in which, at age 27, I finally learned how to drive—navigating the streets of Portland while clutching the steering wheel so hard that I left impressions on my palms.

At first, I drove only on familiar routes. But without being able to clearly see or hear what was going on around me, what had been relaxing back streets by bike became harrowing obstacle courses along which I could barely bring myself to drive as fast as I would pedal.

So I gritted my teeth and took to the bigger roads—the ones I went out of my way to avoid on a bike. It was a revelation of a whole new city. As my mental map adjusted to going twice the speed that I was used to, I regularly overshot my destinations; then, it would take forever to park. Businesses that seemed far apart by bike, cut off from each other by winding routes and bad intersections, would turn out to be only a few blocks apart by car. My usual shortcuts became unavailable, and I had the constant feeling once again of being lost in my own city.

I learned how frustrating it feels to go any less than 20 miles per hour in a car, even if the traffic lights are timed for slower speeds. It was better to stay off such slow streets anyway—in a car, it was easier and faster to drive five miles to the mall than it was to pick my way a third of that distance through local streets to the places I was used to shopping.

I didn't ever get comfortable driving. I'm glad I learned, though. Driving a car taught me new things about my city, and most of all it taught me empathy for the people I share the road with every day. It helped me understand, if not always approve, why drivers do some of the things they do (regular drivers who try out bicycling for the first time often report similar revelations).

Driving in cities is difficult, frustrating, limiting, and scary. No wonder people are stressed, mad, or impatient—or demand faster, wider roads with no bikes on them.

The map of Portland I navigate on two wheels is a much friendlier place, with a richer array of options and fewer frustrations. That didn't happen by accident, and it didn't happen overnight.

Some roads are better suited to cycling than others, but are not always specifically designed and marked to be that way. In cities where bicycling still hasn't made it onto public officials' radar, regular riders use trial and error to find the best routes. They share them with each other informally online, point them out during group rides, and sometimes publish them as unofficial bike maps. Eventually, when the city does begin to invest in cycling, these existing informal routes often get attended to first: sometimes invisibly with safety fixes such as signal-timing adjustments, and other times more boldly with pavement markings and traffic-calming devices.

Whatever form it takes, bicycle infrastructure costs money too. Large projects such as the off-street networks in Houston and Minneapolis can run into the hundreds of millions. That's a lot of dough, and opponents will never let you forget it.

The idea that investing in long-distance bicycle paths is good fiscal management has long been a counterintuitive one in the U.S. Part of the problem, of course, is that bicycle infrastructure isn't taken seriously. It's seen as recreational like a city playground for affluent adults, a boondoggle, or the classic example of pork. People who ride know better, as do their employers, their doctors, the businesses that serve them, and the researchers who keep track of all these gains. Many members of Congress do as well, and the tides are shifting. But in the middle of a funding crisis, every ounce of political capital counts, and bicycling just isn't on the radar yet as a serious transportation option.

When you brush away the rhetoric, though, even the fanciest bikeways are a screaming bargain. For the cost of one freeway interchange, you can completely transform your city and immeasurably improve the wealth, health, and happiness of its citizens. And the more you spend, the better the return on your investment.

Off-road, multi-use paths—paved trails accessible to people biking and walking, but forbidden to cars—cost the most. These can run up to as much as a million dollars per mile—or more. As with infrastructure for cars, any time you have a bridge or an interchange it adds to the bill. The standard model in the U.S. is typically located and designed with recreation in mind. The shared nature of the path becomes awkward once they become commuter corridors—fast two-wheeled vehicles aren't an easy fit with more leisurely strolling. The best of these resemble Copenhagen's new superhighways; they're extra wide and provide clearly marked lanes for different types of use. However, this is extraordinarily rare in the U.S. Most multi-use paths are eight-foot strips of unmarked asphalt, and amenities, such as lighting, air pumps, way-finding signs, and traffic signals, are nearly unheard of.

The type of urban bicycle infrastructure that's taking root in the U.S. is better represented in Chicago: a city that's in the midst of a bike lane extravaganza led by two successive mayors.[44] Chicago has a few multi-use paths, but is focusing instead on separating bikes from moving cars on the city's existing street network. City transportation workers have honed their processes and budgets in order to bring the cost of these new bikeways down considerably.[45]

In 2012, a mile of regular, striped bike lane was estimated to cost $50,000. Buffered bike lanes began going in on extra busy streets, providing extra space between bicycle and car traffic demarcated by painted diagonal stripes. These cost $85,000 per mile. Protected lanes, which are physically separated by either plastic bollards or a line of parked cars, and which often involve separate traffic signals to prevent conflicts at intersections, are the new gold standard in the U.S. for creating space for bicycling on major roads. Experimental protected lanes in other cities have cost as much as a million dollars per mile, with much of this cost going to design and engineering. Chicago prices them at $170,000 to $250,000 per mile.

As relatively cheap as this stuff is to build, bicycle infrastructure really seems like a smart investment when you look beyond its sticker price. Wear and tear on the roads from bicycles is nearly nil—asphalt roads need to be maintained even if nobody travels on them at all (weather makes this a necessity). But the greatest share of the damage done to roads is by cars and trucks, which are getting heavier, and more numerous. On-street bikeways are cheapest to maintain; after all, roads must be swept, restriped, and occasionally resurfaced, with or without bike lanes.[46] And even off-street paths cost less than a freeway project would spend on photocopying in a year.

In the end, anything we do is going to cost money. What's important is that we're able to differentiate between an expense (i.e. something that produces massive debt and crushing external costs) and an investment (i.e. something that returns initial expenditures many times over).

But big changes come slow. And when the budget gets tight, it becomes harder to ask these big-picture questions.

Maybe it's easier to think of roads the way we think of our teeth. When we put off going to the dentist—or filling potholes, which is a widespread occurrence in our country right now—we end up with escalating problems. Like cavities, potholes become deeper and wider the longer they're left alone. Eventually the roadbed becomes compromised. Dabbing a bit of asphalt into a shallow pothole only takes a road crew a few minutes; reconstructing a compromised foundation takes all day and requires far more materials. Hundreds of dollars turn into tens of thousands. This situation is exactly the source of a substantial part of our local and national infrastructure crises.

The City of Portland calculates that preventative maintenance can be 10 times cheaper[47] than rehabilitating a road that has gotten to the point of being in very poor condition. The city's policy is to prioritize putting its money into filling small potholes rather than fixing the worst roads first. On a larger scale, it would be fiscally responsible to do the same thing: invest first in prevention, taking heavy traffic off of streets by whatever means possible. One of the most cost-effective ways to do that is to make room for bicycles.

Bicycle infrastructure projects are all the more appealing because they pencil out, running at a net positive and putting money back into the system at all levels.[48] When someone rides a bicycle, they're saving money. And they're more likely to spend that money at businesses close to home, and are less likely to take unplanned time off work or need expensive medical care. When a street has bike infrastructure, it becomes less polluted and more prosperous. It's a winning situation for everyone.

Large road projects are often funded in a down economy because they create jobs. But roads are actually the least job-intensive of any transportation investment; bikeways are the most, creating more jobs per million dollars spent than road projects because there are so few materials involved that most of the budget goes to workers.[49]

So why do we decry bikeways, which cost very little and produce all sorts of economic benefits, as wasteful, while we're eager to take on vast new debts to build more and wider roads? Relative affordability is part of the problem. Bicycle infrastructure projects are often simply too small to bring powerful backers to the table to lobby for them. And modest proposals to stripe a few bike lanes cost so many millions of dollars cheaper that the increase in jobs doesn't register.

Bicycle advocates are only beginning to realize this. They have long been used to operating in the margins, and are in the habit of asking only for incremental changes and insubstantial sums of money. But history—and Houston—shows that bigger projects succeed better, both in getting built and in serving emerging needs. A bigger vision leaves room for negotiation; a compromise on a large proposal is still better than fully funding of a tiny one.

The federal government only began spending money on active transportation—that is, infrastructure that supports transit, bicycling, and walking—in 1991.[50] An increasing amount of cycling improvements have been paid for in this way in recent years, but the amount spent on non-motorized travel still adds up to less than 2% of the federal transportation budget.[51] Still, this small amount of money has done great things. Since 2006, 250 new miles of bike lanes were installed in New York City, and 80% of the cost was paid for through federal grants.[52] This relatively miniscule investment entirely transformed the city—for the better and more prosperous, as we shall see in future chapters.

Research shows that when federal money flows into bicycle projects, more people start commuting by bicycle—in part because of the projects themselves, and in part because of the ways that funding is used to leverage greater local funding, sometimes from private entities.[53]

City, state, and regional governments have also been at the forefront of retrofitting their communities for bicycling. Municipal budgets for infrastructure and events often are patched together from a variety of sources. Government funds are supplemented or at times exceeded by nonprofit grants from bicycling and livability advocacy organizations as well as private sector funding—occasionally from the bike industry, but more often from health care companies seeking to boost their effectiveness and profile in preventing sedentary diseases.

Federal transportation funding is drying up, and states and cities are not faring much better. As transportation departments retrench to focus on filling potholes, more creative funding solutions will be needed for anything but minimum maintenance. Dollar amounts are going to get smaller, and the impact of those dollars spent will need to reach more people.

Complete Streets ordinances are an example of how civic budgets can be used efficiently, installing bike infrastructure at only marginal costs.[54] These policies require, with more or fewer loopholes, that bicycling and walking infrastructure be added when new streets are built or existing streets are repaired. It's standard for the stripes on city streets to be repainted once or twice a year—and the extra cost to paint two more lines to add a bike lane to a medium-sized, 25-mph street is negligible.

Increasingly, cities incorporate bicycle planning into the process of updating aging sewer systems and updating them with bioswales that absorb storm-water runoff before it can reach the sewer. Their concept of "green streets" is a good fit with the vision of bicycle friendly corridors with signs and signals that mark them as such, and it's a cost-effective solution.[55]

Civic budget shortfalls are also an opportunity for grassroots communities and organizations to take the lead—and we are already seeing that happen.

A local example of creative funding is Pittsburgh, a city that went bankrupt several years ago and where residents are increasingly taking to bikes. Until 2005, the city had lots of people biking around, but a lack of places to park. Bike staples—upside-down U-shaped metal poles—are usually installed either by business owners on their own property, which is hit or miss, or by city governments on public property, which wasn't going to happen. Instead, the local advocacy organization, Bike Pittsburgh, worked with community partners and won grant funding to install hundreds of racks with the iconic three rivers symbol in front of businesses and services throughout the city.

Or take Detroit, another city that is in a financial hole. 2013 will see the installation of 100 miles of bike lanes, an enviable investment for even the most solvent city. Detroit Greenways, a nonprofit organization, is leading the way on paying and planning —with much of the funding coming from the Tour de Troit, a 5,000-person, annual bike ride.

There's no end to creative solutions. And it may be for the best that the leadership for initiating and funding transportation projects is shifting to a more grassroots level.

As bicycle advocates gain allies in political leadership and learn to make civic funding machines work in their favor, we are starting to see that those funds are, like any other, not distributed equitably. As bike lanes start to be seen as a desirable commodity, they are being installed in communities whose residents know how to shake the tree for government support.

Communities that might need such facilities even more badly—as a matter of literal survival rather than success—remain largely out of the loop.

The bicycle advocacy organizations that are beginning to win the money game tend to represent member bases that are largely white and affluent. The result: relatively affluent, white-majority neighborhoods enjoy the economic boost that comes with bike infrastructure. Those who can't keep up with rising property values, and the higher-priced local stores that come with them, move away—often to places that have more transportation restrictions than their neighborhood originally did.

There's always room for advocacy organizations to stop and shift their direction, reaching out to new constituencies and updating their vision and strategic plans to make equity a priority.

But there's always more than enough room for people to take matters into their own hands, whether that means painting our own DIY bike lanes when the city won't step in, launching new organizations and initiatives to give voice to the needs of overlooked communities, or simply getting out there and being visible riding our bicycles together.

If we wait long enough, people will no longer be able to afford to drive or maintain the roads at all. And then we'll see the real DIY solution for crumbling road infrastructure that so many have already taken—putting knobby tires on our bicycles so we can keep on rolling.

•   •   •

I was tying a take-out pizza to the back of my bicycle one summer evening when a guy rushed out of the restaurant to ask about my cargo bike. He was a tourist on a weeklong visit and his excitement about being in Portland was infectious. He, his wife, and their young daughter were visiting for the first time, and he couldn't believe it was all real, just the way he'd been reading about on the Internet for years.

The guy's name was Mike. He worked as a journalist and in his spare time he ran a bike blog called Tucson Velo. At the time, I was working for the Portland blog that had largely inspired his trip and his advocacy. We laughed at the coincidence and exchanged cards. A year later when I was in Tucson, he took me on a tour of the city's nascent bikeway network and told me his story.

It all started on another vacation. Back in 2008, like many visitors to Oceanside, California, Irene and Mike McKisson rented cruisers and pedaled along the beach. It was so much fun that Mike decided he should buy a bike when they got home to Tucson so he could go on weekend rides.

He was in his twenties at the time, but he wasn't exactly at the peak of health and fitness. His job had him sitting in front of a computer all day, and he "ate unhealthy meals—sometimes four of them in a day."[56]

He started to go on rides, often with friends, and had a blast doing it. The problem: he had trouble keeping up. His competitive spirit kicked in and he started to take bicycling seriously, putting in miles everywhere he could get them, including to and from work. He started eating better so he could ride faster. To spur himself on with a concrete goal, he signed up for a 40-mile organized ride, though he was nervous about being able to complete the whole thing.

He made it, and then kept riding. And as he rode, he felt better and better. He'd hardly set out with health in mind, but within six months, he was able to stop taking blood pressure medication. Within a year after that, he sold his car and started his blog to serve as a hub for local bicycle racing, culture, and advocacy. Because of all the bicycling, he felt healthier than ever. Because of the change in his eating habits, he lost so much weight that he had to buy new sets of clothes three times. Because of his blog, he found that he'd gained an influential voice in spurring his city on to build more places to bike and build them right.

A year later, when he signed up for the 100-mile version of that first organized ride, finishing was no question.

When their daughter was born, the McKissons bought an additional car again. But it didn't take long for her to grow big enough to ride gleefully on the back of Mike's long-tail cargo bike. At that point, Irene made an unexpected announcement: She wanted a cargo bike too. After discussing all the logistics, the only sticking point seemed to be storage—with two cars and Mike's bikes, there was no room in the garage.

So they decided to take the biggest weight-loss step of all: They sold their second car and said goodbye to 7,000 pounds of steel and plastic.

"The power of the bike is that it is healthy and a total blast," McKisson told me. "It's not a workout, it's a fun excursion or a cheap way to get somewhere that also happens to burn calories."

Tucson is another sleeper bike city. It's crisscrossed with a rapidly expanding network of trails along which McKisson took many of his early rides. In recent years the city has also made efforts to improve its streets for cycling, painting lanes onto the larger main drags and creating "bike boulevards" by connecting a network of neighborhood streets with safer crossings. It's all impressive, but the real gem is the trail network, called The Loop, which will eventually consist of 130 miles of paved bicycling and walking paths that form a ring around the center of the city.

The Loop, in its partially finished state, has already been an economic boon for the area. It is overseen by the county, which estimates that every dollar spent building it is generating nine dollars worth of economic impact for county residents.[57] By far, the largest part of this economic impact (fully half) is in health costs.

If you ignored all other economic and community benefits of bicycling, the factor of health alone is more than enough reason to invest hundreds of times as much as we currently do into retrofitting our entire country to be a bicycling paradise.

The U.S. has the world's most expensive healthcare system. Our healthcare budget is huge, and growing. It's currently approaching one fifth of our entire GDP—a total of nearly $3 trillion, or over $8,000 per person per year. On a household level alone, health care is breaking the bank. Families pay as much, or more, for health insurance as the high amounts we spend on transportation, and the costs are rising fast.[58]

Yet our health is terrible. In comparison to economically similar countries, all of which spend less than we do on health, we are suffering greatly.[59] But statistics are not necessary to make this point. Walk down a street, or into a mall or an office building anywhere in the U.S. and you'll see it. Our bodies are struggling, and our spirits are low. We, as a people, do not feel well.

This is not because we need to spend more money, but because we desperately need to do things differently.

Physical activity is one of those things. It isn't enough on its own—we also need to eat better. But it's a big piece, and a proven one. Sitting for long periods of time—even if you exercise regularly—is just about the worst thing you can do for your health, increasing your risk of death by all causes by 50%.[60] In terms of your total lifespan, lack of daily physical activity is one of the most truly dangerous activities you can do any day; certainly far more dangerous than riding a bicycle.[61] Most of us simply don't move around enough during the course of a day. When we are active, we fare better, in our health and in our bank accounts.

We've all heard that we need to exercise more. But having grown up in suburbia, I don't believe that the majority of people eat unhealthy food, drive everywhere, and sit all day out of laziness. It is a product of their environments and transportation. Time spent driving is strongly correlated with today's chronic diseases.[62] But that correlation is still strong when you ignore how people travel and look at where they live.

However much time we spend in the car, though, fewer than a third of us in the U.S. meet the CDC's minimum requirements for healthy physical activity—30 minutes a day, five days a week.

We are far more likely to achieve this requirement simply by hopping on a bike for short trips than by undertaking expensive and time-consuming endeavors such as a regimen of exercise classes or membership at a gym. Bicycling is one of those lifestyle habits that doesn't usually even feel like exercise but can hold a whole host of diseases at bay. Adults who regularly commute by bike have the average fitness of someone ten years younger. They also enjoy improved blood pressure, insulin levels, cholesterol levels, less risk of some cancers, heart disease, and diabetes, and, overall, longer lives.

But as far as how to actually figure out bicycling or any other solution, we're often on our own, and in a hostile environment to boot. When it comes to public health, unlike traffic congestion, it's all about managing demand.

The national discourse about health focuses far more on problematic metrics like body weight rather than policies and environmental factors that can either limit or expand our choices. The so-called obesity epidemic is made up of a number of chronic diseases, some of which have been found to correlate with body weight; but the size of our streets is much more to blame in causing them than the size of our bodies.

Take food deserts—places where grocery stores and healthy food are few and far between. Food deserts exist in any kind of place: urban, suburban, or rural. They're both a cause and a result of the breathtaking inequities built into the pattern of our streets. Grocery stores are particularly hard to find in low-income neighborhoods. In many, liquor stores are far more prevalent, as are corner stores that stock only highly-processed, packaged foods that are extremely caloric, full of carcinogens, and high in saturated fats—the kinds of food that make you feel crappy all day and die young. Without a car, it's difficult to get to larger grocery stores; access to affordable, healthy food is a major reason many families cite for needing to own a car.

Food isn't the only factor that can make or break a neighborhood's health. Your chances of chronic disease rise greatly the more isolated you are from destinations like jobs, stores, and schools. Places that have little street life and are felt to be unsafe are also strongly correlated with chronic diseases like diabetes because of the simple fact that it's unpleasant or scary to walk there.[63, 64]

This is sometimes a matter of unsafe infrastructure and too-fast traffic, but calming cars does not unilaterally improve the social life of the street. Studies that look at access to parks in different communities have found that even when there is no racial disparity in walkability in the built environment, other barriers can exist, such as violence, harrassment, and the quality of destinations like parks.[65] Gang violence is a deterrent to street life in many neighborhoods. Similarly, the threat of surveillance and violence by police can discourage walking, bicycling, or making use of public spaces. Adding bike lanes doesn't fix this problem, and in practice it too often comes as part of a package that includes the wholesale displacement of residents.

A dismal study in Toronto found that people living in bleak neighborhoods, on the city's fringes, that didn't have sidewalks, and abutted highways—and that were cut off from grocery stores and social gathering places—were likely to die, on average, 20 years younger than those living in the affluent, relatively walkable and bicycle-accessible downtown core.[66]

The main reason for this greatly reduced lifespan: diabetes.

Type II Diabetes is the preventable form of the disease. It used to be known as "adult onset diabetes" but so many children have been diagnosed with it in recent years that the term has fallen out of use. It's estimated that 6% of the world's adult population has this disease, though cases are nearly all in the so-called developed or developing world. In the U.S., the rate of diagnosed diabetes is 9% of adults,[67] wuich is up from 3.5% in 1980. People who are Asian American, African American, and descended from some Latin American and Native American areas are nearly twice as likely to suffer from the disease as non-Hispanic white people.

Diabetes is the seventh leading cause of death in the U.S., and is related to other serious conditions such as heart disease, strokes, limb amputations, kidney failure, and blindness. Its treatment is expensive and time consuming; the increasing number of people who suffer from it are often not able to support themselves by working and must rely on public assistance, particularly Medicare. By one account, Medicare treatment of patients with the disease accounts for 3.5% of the national budget—more than what is allocated to transportation.[68] You could build a whole lot of bikeways for that amount of money—enough to provide access to every neighborhood in the country.

What causes Type II Diabetes? Genetics loads the gun; environmental factors pull the trigger. They include stress, poor nutrition (particularly massive consumption of sugar), and lack of physical exercise. More recent studies have also found a causative link between diabetes and inhaling fine particulate air pollution—the type that is thickest in low-income neighborhoods next to freeways and major roads. In truth, all of these factors appear together with such frequency that it's hard to know which causes any particular malady. But we do know that by tackling them all at the root we can save lives. The top strategies recommended for preventing the onset of diabetes are changing one's diet and increasing physical activity.

So, the $2-trillion question is: Can access to bicycling solve the health care crisis? The answer is a partial yes, so long as it's being done as part of a package aimed at serving existing residents rather than displacing them.

On a personal level, hopping on a bike can save your life if a bicycle, as well as decent streets to ride on, are available to you. Fortunately, Americans want to ride bikes, and a large number of us already own them. And like McKisson, many of us find the joy of bicycling to transcend our self-consciousness about our bodies and the negative and uncomfortable associations many of us have with exercise for its own sake.

But many people who want to bike tend to balk at the prospect of it, and reasonably so. We've literally built the physical activity out of our environment; in fact, we've created communities where moving about under your own power is penalized, where every incentive urges us to do otherwise. It behooves all of us to make sure that option is not just theoretically available if we want it, but attractive and convenient, laid down in paint and pavement, for ourselves and for our community.

When we build it, we'll come ride on it. This is particularly apt when a barrier is lifted. In Charleston, South Carolina, when a major highway bridge was recently built—one of the most expensive infrastructure investments in the state—no bicycling or walking facilities were planned at all. Advocates objected and a diverse coalition formed to add a bike and walking path to one side of the bridge. Political leaders balked at the cost, at first, but ended up glad they had made the investment. The new path over the bridge has proven to be immensely popular for both transportation and fun. Two thirds of the users of the new path overall, and 85% of African American users, said that its presence caused them to become more active and get more daily exercise.[69] What's more, path construction created 525 jobs and significantly increased the number of customers at local bike shops.

One analysis of the health savings resulting from the bicycle infrastructure in Portland came up with stunning results. If the city built out only the infrastructure it currently plans to (and it has big plans), it would break even by 2015. By continuing at the same rate, Portland could save $600 million in healthcare costs by 2030. And that doesn't even begin to quantify the value of people having longer, active lives.

In Tucson, Portland, and just about every case where the return on investment for bicycle infrastructure, or even city-sponsored events, has been calculated, the savings in health costs alone is consistent: four or five dollars saved to every one that is spent.[70] Bicycle infrastructure makes so much economic sense that it can accurately be described as a health investment as much as it's a transportation one.

One thing the health care crisis is teaching us is that the basis of our economy isn't the dollar; it's us. The economic health of our communities relies on our ability to participate in them, by working, buying, selling, and helping provide each others' basic needs. The best investment we can make—personally and as a society—is in the ability to live our lives and live them well.

Bikes may not be able to solve our health care crisis singlehanded. And they won't eliminate the political and economic machinations that continue to deepen it. But bicycling is one of the rare areas where people can directly and concretely address our own health and the health of our community, and quickly see big results. In this light, bicycling for transportation isn't so much a lifestyle choice as it's a form of civic action.

The topic of mental health has been losing some of its stigma in recent years, and as a result has begun to be treated similarly to physical illnesses— both as well and as poorly.

We, as a society, feel physically unwell and incapable, we are anxious and depressed, and the environments where we spend our time do not provide us with our basic needs or inspire us. These factors support each other in a vicious cycle, and contribute to a sense that we are not in enough control of our lives to do anything about either.

Just as with some physical illnesses, too much focus on treating particular mental health symptoms can be to the detriment of people who might benefit more from a preventative approach.[71] And as with physical health, one of the best ways to prevent some of the most prevalent mental ailments today is exercise.

While it's rather quaint to say that exercise is good for your mind and emotions, science is finding exactly that. Even a few minutes of very moderate exercise has a strong positive effect on mood, to the extent that prescribing exercise is even becoming a standard practice of psychologists. Being able to build exercise into your routine is a benefit on a number of levels, from helping you deal with stress to improving your confidence to helping you sleep better to just plain making you happy.

Happiness has a mythos about it in our culture, but a pragmatic way of looking at it is as the absence of, or ability to deal well with, stress. Besides making us unhappy, stress is an aggravating factor in just about every mental and physical disease there is, particularly the chronic ones that we are struggling with in the U.S. today. The vast majority of us regularly feel unduly stressed out,[72] particularly those who live in poverty.

In economics, happiness is conveniently measured in units. We expect that money can create more happiness units. A standard finding in the science of happiness is that this is true for those living in poverty. Once your income rises above subsistence level, earning yet more money still makes you happier, but in much smaller increments and not nearly as much as having strong family and social relationships. And the diminishing returns continue; once you move beyond a middle-class income, they nearly dry up entirely.

The primary causes of unhappiness? Having a bad commute. If you have a job, the drive there is the most stressful thing you'll do on any given day.[73] And people with particularly long car commutes are more likely to be depressed, have a mental health breakdown, and even get divorced.[74]

Just how widespread is our happiness problem? Here's an indicator: one in ten adults in the U.S. meets the diagnostic criteria for depression.[75] Even worse, suicide rates have been rising for the past decade, after declining in the nineties. Sprawl doesn't help—teen suicides increase significantly in less densely populated areas.[76] This may be related to the increasing poverty of the suburbs, which is also correlated with mental health problems and higher suicide rates.

Urban or suburban, another primary cause of unhappiness is social isolation and the lack of a social support network. A groundbreaking study in 1969 in San Francisco found that children living on busy roads had fewer friends (on average, the kids on the busiest roads reported having fewer than one friend). A more recent study in the U.K. looked at adults' social circles and found similar results. People who live on busier roads had 75% fewer friends than those in quieter neighborhoods.[77]

Why? Among the adults, traffic noise is a major factor, said the study authors, as are health from air pollution, and people's likelihood of spending time in front of their houses and letting their children play outdoors.

By contrast, bicycling is overwhelmingly likely to make you happy. Study after study shows that bicycling—or similar exercise—reduces stress, improves mental health and self-esteem, and has an antidepressant effect. People who bicycle and walk to work are more likely than drivers or transit users to report that they like their commutes.[78] A 2011 study of bicycle commuters found that they're simply happier than people who drive or take transit to work: they have less stress, and report that they feel freedom, relaxation, and excitement in their daily lives.[79]

Despite its upsides, bicycling can be a source of stress, especially in heavy traffic without facilities or other people to ride with. This may be partially mitigated by the positive effects of riding. But the best way to solve that problem is to make our streets better places so we all have the opportunity to live better, longer, and happier lives.

Learning
to Share

(5)

One of the most creative economic solutions for making bicycling accessible and spurring infrastructure development is at once simple and counterintuitive: give people bicycles.

In March 2013, I visited Washington, DC for a conference and stayed with my friend Anna. The last time I visited had been several years before. She had lived far from downtown but was a few blocks from a Metro station, so I had taken the subway everywhere I needed to go. She now lives in a much closer-in neighborhood. There's a Metro station less than half a mile from her new house, but I didn't set foot in it once.

I didn't need to. Only five blocks away, there was a kiosk holding up to 12 Capital Bikeshare (CaBi) bikes. I could stroll over, swipe a borrowed key, pull out a bike, ride it downtown to another docking station, and walk to my conference in less time than it would have taken to walk to the subway station and wait for the next train to roll in.

Over the next week, I used bike-share nearly every day. At first, it was hard to find the docking stations, and I would waste time walking around looking for one to return my bike to. I learned that there would always be one right next to a Metro station entrance; anywhere else, all I needed to do was ask a passerby, and they could point me the way.

I also had trouble finding good bike routes, and ended up on some streets that I would have preferred to avoid. But the impatient DC drivers I remember seem to have learned to watch out for confused-looking tourists on heavy, red bicycles. As I learned my way around the city's brand new network of bike lanes and boulevards, people gave me a broad berth.

The bikes themselves are slow, heavy, and always a little out of tune. I minded this at first, frustrated that I couldn't ride as fast as I wanted to. Maybe it was a matter of getting comfortable with the handling. Maybe it was finding my way to those mellower bike routes, where a slow roll doesn't seem as poky by comparison to the cars going by. Or maybe it was after I'd seen enough fellow CaBi riders with huge grins plastered across their faces.

Whatever it was, I soon stopped missing my own bike and started enjoying myself immensely.

I definitely didn't miss the frustrating routine of having to remember locks and lights when I went out the door—or the pain in the neck that ensues when I forget. Bike-share steeds have built-in lights that shine when you pedal, and as they are only intended for short trips from kiosk to kiosk, there's no need to lock them.

Capital Bikeshare in DC is a typical example of its genre. Members pay an annual fee that nets them a red key that they can use to check out any bike. They then have half an hour to pedal where they need to go and securely park the bike at another station. Nonmembers, like tourists, can check out the bikes by swiping a credit card. Seven bucks earns you as many 30-minute rides as you can squeeze into the next 24 hours. The bikes are meant for short hops only—keeping one over the time limit adds sizable fees—but you can make as many 30-minute trips as you need to. You can ride to a museum or a restaurant, and then dock your bike. When you're ready to head somewhere else, you check out another bike from the same kiosk or a different one, and then move on.

Modern bike-share systems are a far cry from the free "yellow bike" programs of past decades, which consisted of bicycles that were simply painted a distinctive color and left lying unlocked around a city for anyone to use. In general, those idealistically deployed steeds quickly became integrated into the underground economy, inevitably concluding their short lives at the bottom of a river or lake.

In 2005, the first modern bike-share system was launched: the *Vélo'v* program in Lyon, France. With its secure, credit-card-operated docking system and its clever funding mechanism (an advertising company pays for the system in exchange for billboard rights throughout the city), it became the inspiration and prototype for similar systems in cities around the world.

It first caught on in European cities, most notably Paris, a city where one of the main barriers to bicycling had been the predominance of multi-story apartment buildings without elevators or storage space. The *Vélib'* bike-share system caught on like wildfire. Paris, which had not previously been famous for being very bicycle friendly, scrambled to catch up with the demand, hastily adding bike lanes where none had been before. Overnight, the city became a place to ride a bicycle: 250,000 Parisians are now members of the system, making over 100,000 daily trips on the bikes.

Bike-share started small in North America in 2008, with a tiny but successful program in one area of Washington, DC that was a precursor to today's CaBi system. In 2009, Montreal launched a large program that is largely credited with that city's rise to one of the best cycling cities on the continent, if not the world. In 2010, Denver and Minneapolis opened their bike-share kiosks for business. After that, bike-share fever hit, and it became hard to count the cities jumping on board.

The effect of a new bike-share system launch is instant and transformative. Bicycling becomes a form of public transportation; crowds of new bike commuters, tourists, and errand-runners carve out space for themselves and each other on the roads, producing the visibility and demand needed to spur political leaders to create safer, more comfortable streets for cycling. And bike-share solves two age-old problems of bike ownership: theft (the company takes the risk, not the rider) and flat tires (if your borrowed bike flats, you simply walk it to a nearby kiosk and check out a new one).

The next generation of bike-share is already here. Smaller-scale systems without kiosks, many run on open source software, are being tested at universities and companies with sprawling campuses. Doing away with kiosks makes these programs infinitely cheaper to run. The bikes are sturdy and easily adjustable and have a built-in GPS locator and a lock. To use the system, you ask an app on your phone or computer to tell you where to find the nearest bike. When you select a bike, you are given a code to unlock it. You go find the bike—locked to a pole or a rack, wherever the last person to use it left it—ride where you need to go, lock it up, and let your app know that you're done. Maybe it's there for you on the way back, or maybe you find another bike close by.

Where it is installed, bike-share reduces the already low price of admission for cycling and breaks down many barriers for would-be cyclists. Using a shared bike isn't free, but it's far less of a commitment than buying a bicycle. Riding a bike-share bike might be more work physically than riding one of your own, but you need less mental and logistical preparation if you're totally new to it. A purchased bike doesn't come with a map, lights, or instruction manual, while bike-share comes with all three. And the results are manifest;

when these programs launch, the streets fill with bikes. Moreover, in many cities, bike-share use is divided nearly 50/50 between men and women, a far cry from the typical cycling gender gap.

The programs are so functional, in part, because they treat bicycles more like transit than like personal vehicles. The kiosks' placement near bus stops and train stations makes both cycling and transit function better. Transit suffers from what planners call "the last mile problem"—it can take you wherever you need to go but only up to a point, and that point grows farther from your destination as development marches outward. Bike-share is proving effective at bridging that gap, making a two-mile trip to the nearest train stop feasible and fun rather than a good reason to drive the car across the city.

In 2013, over 500 cities around the world boasted wildly successful bike-share programs. The only systems that have not done well are in Australia, where helmet use is mandatory and strictly enforced.

DC's bike-share system was built by leveraging federal funding, but its fee structure is working. Now it has the dubious distinction of being the only transit system in the country to break even, with all operating costs coming from user fees. This news is hopeful and, in many ways, positive. But it shows the fatal flaw of free-market perspectives on transportation economics.

After Denver's bike-share program launched in 2010, initial research found that 90% of its members were Caucasian. A city councilor who represents a largely Latino district in West Denver asked publicly why no bike-share stations had been built in his district. His constituents had extremely high rates of sedentary diseases, he said, and they both wanted and needed access to bicycles. He was told that due to funding constraints, stations could only be placed in areas where they would make the most money—and his district was definitely not one of those places.[80]

Denver is not alone. In diverse Washington, DC, 81% of bike-share members are white, and most are of above average income. Boston is similar.

Not all bike-sharing systems are run as for-profit enterprises; most are run by nonprofits or government agencies. But the bottom line is always a factor, and for that reason, people of color or those with low incomes all too often just don't have access. Kiosks aren't placed in their neighborhoods, or the streets just aren't bike friendly enough to want to use them. And most bike-share systems require a credit card or a several-hundred-dollar hold on one's bank account. One in twelve households in the U.S. are unbanked, making bike-share—and the benefits of convenience, mobility, and health that come with it—immediately inaccessible to a large portion of the populace.

Other problems have emerged within the bike-share business. The programs are labor-intensive. Natural bike-share usage patterns rarely leave an ideal distribution of bikes, or open rack spaces, and bikes must be constantly "balanced" by workers who load bikes from a full kiosk onto a truck and redistribute them throughout the service area. The bikes must also be maintained, which requires staff time as well. In 2013, the Department of Labor opened an investigation in response to allegations that employees of the system were not being paid federally mandated wages or benefits. CaBi was at that time run by Alta Bike share on a contract from the District government, which had built-in compensation requirements, and eighteen current and former employees said that they were owed $100,000 in unpaid wages.[81] In late 2014, amid concerns about the rollout and management of the CitiBike bike-share system in New York City, Alta Bike share was sold; the new owners promised to improve operations, cut costs, and expand service.[82] But it seems likely that hopes for bike-share as a silver bullet, break-even solution have met the ultimate reality check: transportation as a utility that serves the public comes with the same labor, logistics, and equity requirements as any other transportation system.

• • •

I attended the National Bike Summit for the first time in 2013. This is bicycle advocacy's main event: Every March since 2001, advocates from around the country come to share their progress and setbacks, learn from each other, and lobby their congressional representatives for the local and national advancement of bicycling.

At an after party, I talked with two delegates from Recycle-a-Bicycle, an advocacy organization and community bike shop based in New York City. Karen Overton, the organization's founder and original director, shared that at the first Bike Summit she attended, a decade ago, she was one of 20 women. "Maybe not even twenty," she amended, "at a 700-person event."

The organization's current executive director Pasqualina Azzarello nodded. She had first attended the Bike Summit four years ago, she said, and had counted only ten other people of color.

In 2013, the balance began to tip. The League of American Bicyclists had launched programs in the last year aimed at reaching out to women and people of color, and the results at the Summit were visible in the mixing crowds of advocates.

At the 2012 Summit, the League had hosted a smaller women's forum the day before. Sixty people attended a two-hour-long program and it was counted as a success. The next year, the women's event drew hundreds of participants to a daylong conference. Most, though not all, were women. Many attendees had come out for the Leagues' newly minted Equity Advisory Council, which had convened for the first time the night before. There was a palpable excitement in the air; people clearly were inspired to be among so many fellow advocates, often for the first time. Many stayed for the Summit, bringing the first event's energy and diversity along with them.

Other people had told me that the Bike Summit had always been 90% or more middle-aged white men, and I had assumed they were exaggerating. But looking around during the event, I realized they were probably understating matters.

For my own part, I'd never attended before. The cost of the trip and the event was prohibitive, and though I was aware that it would be a smart place to learn and connect, I shied away. In cycling circles I'd already had plenty of experience being one of only a few women in the room, and the Summit just seemed like an expensive opportunity to be sidelined.

I went that year only because someone at the League had reached out personally and invited me. That exact same reason seemed, in fact, to be the motivation of many first-time attendees—they had simply been asked. By the conversations I overheard and the light in peoples' eyes, I knew they too were finding the experience valuable: the sessions, the networking, and the feeling of being a welcome part of a growing and increasingly successful movement.

Still, I didn't attend the lobbying day after the conference. Talking to congressional leaders didn't seem like my strong suit, and I wanted to explore the city using bike-share. Afterwards, looking at photos online, I had regrets—it turned out that I wasn't the only one who had taken a step back. In the pictures, it was all back to business as usual, a Senator posing for a picture with a state delegation made up of nine out of 10 white men in suits.

Why such a gap between those who needed an invitation and those who already thought of themselves as part of the club? To understand it helps to look at some history.

Kittie Knox was a 21-year-old Bostonian seamstress and a member of the Riverside Bicycle Club, the country's first African American cycling club. Knox and her fellow club members went on rides and performed graceful two wheeled feats. Knox won awards for the cycling outfits she made for herself, even though the knickerbockers she favored were scandalous attire for a woman at the time.

This was in the 1890s—the first golden age of bicycling. The League of American Wheelmen was the country's premier bicycle organization. It was formed for two main purposes: to lobby for good, paved roads and to oversee the wildly popular sport of bicycle racing.

Knox joined the League in 1893. The next year the organization passed a "color bar," a rule stating that only white people could be members or participate in sanctioned bicycle races. The rule had been highly contested within the organization's ranks, and was voted in narrowly after furious debates.

The following year, Knox made plans to attend the League's annual meeting. The debate continued. Would her preexisting membership be honored, or did the color bar effectively revoke her privileges as a League member? It was never settled, but she went anyway. Accounts of what happened next vary; one newspaper reported that she was ejected from the event, but Knox herself claimed that she was welcomed graciously.[83]

The League disbanded soon after; it had split into two groups—a motoring arm and a cycling arm—but neither flourished. It reformed later in the century, eventually changing its name to its present, more inclusive variant: The League of American Bicyclists. In 1999, League President Earl Jones removed the color bar from the books and issued a formal apology for that ill-conceived rule.[84]

If you were to only read the cultural coverage of bicycling in the national daily newspapers, you'd think that the people riding now are all young and white, with liberal arts degrees, who work at hip coffee shops or mobile tech startups.[85] Or you might see that the established advocates are lawyers in team kits, powerful white men who treat their ride to work like a training race, or who undertake "supercommutes" of 50 miles or more. There's no denying that many people fitting both descriptions have taken up bicycling and formed clubs and organizations with others who look and ride like them. And it isn't so strange either that these are often the folks who find their way into conversations with reporters.

But who is leading the charge in the bicycle movement today? It's increasingly the people who you don't read about in the style section. New energy and leadership is coming from communities that have the most to lose in our troubled transportation economy, have the least access to mainstream sources of power, and have the most reason to be frustrated with the sluggish pace of change.

Cyclists have long been represented, in research and in lobbying delegations to Congress alike, as middle-aged, professional white men.[86] Many employees at bicycle advocacy organizations are women, but their directors and board are more likely to be men. Bicycle advisory committees are mostly made up of men[87] and most traffic engineers are men.[88] Only community bicycle projects—many of which primarily are composed of and serve people of color—tend to avoid this gaping disparity in their organizational composition.

Bicycling didn't cause the gap in equity in this country. Rather, it reflects the problems of broader society. But bicycling does represent an opportunity for change.

Today, there is a myth that people of color do not like bicycling and do not want the sort of infrastructure changes that make cycling more appealing. Despite a long history of discrimination and unequal access, this has never been widely true, and today the barriers are coming down rapidly, thanks in part to the growing inclusivity of traditional bicycle advocates, but in much larger part to the efforts and leadership of a growing number of grassroots social and advocacy groups.

Events in the League's more recent history are relatable to many advocates working on a wide range of issues that touch on social justice. The organization received funding for and launched an equity initiative and hired Dr. Adonia Lugo to manage it in November 2013.[89] In early 2014, the organization launched a new vision statement, appending the words "for everyone" to its previous vision of "creating a bicycle friendly America." For a while, all seemed to be going well. Reports were written, organizations around the country were reached out to, and national events were held with keynote speakers and panelists who were decidedly not the usual suspects. But all wasn't well under the surface. On March 6, 2015, Lugo resigned. Shortly after she left, I interviewed her for a video project about the initiative. The lack of internal support she had received, she said, had been shocking, and she had actually been prevented from doing the work she was hired to do, making the League a more inclusive and equitable organization. In an interview that same week, (shortly before he also resigned for apparently different reasons), President Andy Clarke said that the idea of making equity a primary concern of the organization was something that the League's board and membership just weren't ready for yet.[90]

Just as neighborhoods where people of color live are often passed over by the type reforms that benefit the community, when amenities do go in, they're all too often treated as development tools with the goal of raising property values and attracting young, professional newcomers to move in. As a result, longtime residents and renters often find themselves priced out of their own neighborhood—replaced by comparatively well-off white people. That this practice produces bitterness is understandable. That bicycling comes to represent it is a shame.

In Portland, the divide is especially strong. Bike around town long enough and you'll see an ethnically diverse mix of fellow riders, especially along the eastern and northern edges of town where our world-famous bike infrastructure makes only rare appearances. But head to any advocacy, industry, or bike culture event and it's a sea of white.

This gap in inclusion has come to a head in the past few years. The Albina neighborhood in Portland's north quadrant was known 50 years ago as "The Black Downtown," a vibrant and bustling business district. But the hospital in the neighborhood wanted to add a new wing, and they wanted the land right in the core of the district. Community activists fought back and lost. The land was claimed, and the theater, music halls, and restaurants at the heart of the neighborhood were torn down.

And then nothing happened.

The new wing of the hospital fell through, and the land sat empty for decades. The neighborhood around it failed to thrive until an urban renewal district was born. A light-rail line was built to the neighborhood. Newcomers could, and did, get assistance buying houses and opening increasingly upscale businesses. Police started responding more promptly to calls from the area, and enforcing complaints against such grievous crimes as African American youth hanging out on their blocks and playing music.

Property values rose, and rents right along with them. Around the time that long time residents were deciding life would be more affordable on the outskirts of town, bike lanes started going in. A handful of people protested— they had always been protesting, but this time it was heard—and the dialogue that resulted didn't show the city at its best. Neighborhood activists put their feet down, wanting to know where the bike lanes and other civic investments were when the neighborhood was mostly African American, and why they were coming here instead of to the new neighborhoods where many of their neighbors had moved. Bicycle advocates responded that race and social justice were irrelevant issues in the neighborhood's bikeway expansion, that the bike lanes would help everyone in the neighborhood and that it was counterproductive to stand in their way. The funding was allocated and the conversation was over, but the simmering resentments, as well as their justifications, remained.[91]

Similar stories have played out all over the country. It's a microcosm of our thinking about car transportation; bikeways, like roads, are used as tools to attract development, and also to sort out what sort of people get to live where.

But the health, economic, and environmental benefits of bicycling are hardly lost on communities who are not on the receiving end of this meager largesse.

Slowing
Things
Down

6

"Get off the road!" At least, I think that's what the woman yelled at me. Her face, as she leaned out her window while she passed me on the right, was stretched into a distorted grimace, and what came out was more of a garbled howl than decipherable language. I've heard those words enough times before, though—or their more profane variations—to get the gist.

It's not as though I was in her way. In downtown Portland, the streetlights are timed at about 13 miles per hour, a reasonable speed by bicycle. When riding there, I'm usually able to pace myself so I can catch what traffic engineers call "the green wave," sailing through each light a couple of seconds after it turns green, without ever having to stop or slow down.

I was keeping pace with the lights that day, which is why, after she passed me, the yelling woman immediately had to stop and wait at a red light. I passed her a moment later when the light turned green, as she was just beginning to accelerate. She gunned it to pass me again . . . and then had to wait again.

For all the grumbling that goes on about how cyclists think we're above the law, nothing seems to infuriate my fellow road users as much as when I'm pedaling straightforwardly and legally on the road, at the same speed as car traffic—or faster.

Savvier motorists see what I'm up to after a block or two and match their pace to mine, catching the greens along with me. Sometimes they smile or lift a hand from the steering wheel in acknowledgment as we roll side-by-side. But every time I go downtown, at least one impatient soul is convinced that I'm holding them up. And they don't mind letting me know that they would prefer I be on the sidewalk (which is illegal in downtown Portland) or on a bike path (which exist in Portland but regrettably don't go to my dentist's office or the grocery store), or squeezed all the way over to the right next to the parked cars (danger!).

I get it, I do. They're stressed, I'm in front of them, they didn't get the memo about traffic signal timing, and maybe this is the last straw on an already frustrating day.

When I read letters to the editor about how cyclists cause traffic jams and increase air pollution, I sometimes wonder if the letter writer is thinking of an encounter like this.

While I ride away, I often think about how I would respond, given the chance. Would I explain the law, the logistics, the common sense of it all? Would I shout right back at them? Would I turn red and stammer? None of the yellers stop to chat, so it's impossible to know.

In reality, what happens all too often is funniest of all: A driver passes me only to stop directly in front of me at a red light just before it turns green. I have to hit the brakes and wait until they can get back up to speed and let traffic flow freely again. By the time I get rolling again I often miss the next light . . . as does the person driving more or less patiently behind me.

Everyone loves to hate traffic congestion. It is by far the least devastating yet most talked about external cost of our current transportation system. Whole television and radio programs are devoted to traffic snarls, and a slow commute is the one transportation issue guaranteed to activate the general public.

Traffic congestion is best understood in economic terms. As anyone who has been stuck in traffic can attest, space on the road is a scarce resource. Our economy is organized around the assumption that access to this limited resource is a right, something we do not need to pay for. As a result, costly as they are to build, nearly all of our streets and highways can be used for free. Except on a toll road, as long as you bring your own vehicle, the roads are "free."

The result is predictable: The demand for road space exceeds the supply. Just as predictably, this leads to the rapid deterioration of the common resource and perennial trouble figuring out how to pay to maintain it. It's a classic example of the tragedy of the commons—when everybody wants to use something, it becomes less useful for everyone. If we were talking about a popular Christmas toy instead, we might predict rioting—and that assessment is not far off the daily reality of and general discourse about our roadways.

The term for this phenomenon is "induced demand." By building a road and inviting the world to use it freely, we are in essence managing the demand for the road in a way that maximizes congestion.

More effective demand management strategies exist, like congestion pricing—reducing demand by charging market rates for the use of a road.

Congestion pricing has not yet come to the United States, though. New York City failed to pass what would essentially be a toll to drive a car or truck into the most traffic-jammed parts of the city during peak hours. But the strategy is working in London, Stockholm, Milan, and Singapore to keep city streets moving during peak hours.

There are other ways to affect demand as well. People in cities all over the world are happy to use a well-run transit system, if it is available, or to ride bicycles if the option is attractive, or a combination of the two.

Induced demand also works for bicycling in the same way as it does for cars. When you build bike paths and lanes, or, more subtly, design streets to be attractive places to bike, people drag their dusty bikes out of the garage and ride.

When it comes to bicycling, short trips, close to home, are the lowest-hanging fruit. A quarter of all our daily travel is done within a mile of our homes. We do most of these short hops by car; less car-centric standards for neighborhood roads could easily make bicycling or walking a more attractive option. This need becomes especially clear when you know that these short local trips result in 60% of the pollution caused by our cars.

One of the worst dangers to our health and well-being in any urban or suburban area—or on any road—is the inevitability of breathing in the fine particles emitted by fuel-burning cars. This particulate matter, which hovers in the air and is absorbed into our systems through our lungs, is worse for our health than cigarette smoke and less avoidable.

All the starting and stopping of traffic congestion is a key ingredient to air pollution. That was the rationale for a four year long injunction against building any new bicycle infrastructure in San Francisco. In 2006, the city passed a moderately-ambitious bicycle plan and was getting ready to start creating a connection of bikeways. A local activist, a 65 year old on a decades-long mission to combat the city's "tacit PC ideology," seized the moment and sued the city. He was successful in convincing the judge to sign an injunction—not a single bicycle lane could be striped or parking staple could be installed until the city could prove that its bike plan would not cause catastrophic pollution by creating more traffic congestion. The environmental review took four years, cost a million dollars,[92] and clocked in at 1,353 pages. When it passed in 2010 and the injunction was lifted, the city was ready—San Francisco gained miles of bikeways overnight.

Did this cause more traffic congestion? It may have, though the environmental plan created strategies to mitigate it, mostly by changing traffic signal timing.

Is traffic congestion a bad thing, though? Yes and no.

Car exhaust is no laughing matter. Nearly half of residents in major urban areas in North America live close enough to highways and other large roads to experience serious problems as a result. Exposure to car emissions worsens and may cause asthma and other lung conditions, including lung cancer. There is evidence to suggest that it leads to hardening of the arteries and thence to heart disease. One study has found an increased risk of heart attacks while in traffic, either while driving or using public transportation. Breathing car exhaust may increase the risk of developing diabetes; it is certain, however, that people who have diabetes suffer disproportionately from the effects of air pollution.[93]

The worst effects of breathing polluted air are experienced where it is densest: in traffic. Spending time on and near highways, freeways, and other busy roads is terrible for your health. How near is a question that is still being studied, but researchers believe that the effects are worst within either a fifth or a third of a mile. People in cars or buses are exposed to considerably more air pollution, perhaps because of, rather than despite, being in a closed space. People walking and bicycling on or next to roads breathe more air, but inhale somewhat less pollution and cyclists have been found to have even less risk if they are on paths that are separated from the road.[94]

The burdens that come with air pollution are, as with so much else, not evenly distributed. Poverty and ethnicity are both major factors that determine the amount of car exhaust we breathe. Children are particularly at risk, beginning before birth. Air pollution affects prenatal development, and a recent study suggests that exposure to air pollution such as diesel particulates, mercury, and lead may put a child at risk for autism.[95] A separate study found double the rate of autism among children who live within 1,000 feet of a freeway in several major cities. Air pollution has also been linked, tentatively, to hyperactivity in kids and childhood cancers. And kids who have high daily exposure to car exhaust score lower on intelligence tests and have more depression, anxiety, and attention problems.[96] This isn't just a matter of where children live—one in three public schools in the U.S. are within a quarter mile of a highway, well within the danger zone.[97]

Traffic jams and air pollution are often talked about at once, as though one inevitably causes the other, and that by fixing one you can also solve the other.

It doesn't quite work that way.

When a road has heavy traffic, more pollution hovers around it. Again, we tackle this problem in every way possible from the supply side, with regulations on tailpipe technology, and subsidies for hybrid and electric cars. And we try to solve pollution in the same way we deal with congestion—by building bigger roads. The current federal transportation bill explicitly offers clean air funds to pay for road widening projects that can show reduced congestion—no matter how faulty the long-term assumptions.

But even the short-term congestion relief—a few minutes each day—doesn't fix pollution. When people can drive faster, they drive farther.[98] Induced demand means that if a road does its job as a development tool, the long term impact of pollution—both on that road and on surface streets that it feeds into—goes up astronomically.[99] These short-term reprieves amount to expensive long-term investments in much greater air quality problems, as the freeway projects of the past have demonstrated.

Also, slow traffic doesn't necessarily mean more pollution. Hyper-milers—people who compete to eke the best gas mileage possible out of their cars—know this well. You burn the least fuel, and thus pollute the least, when you drive at a slow speed, providing a steady flow of gas to the engine or, even better, coasting.[100] The biggest cause of pollution is the traffic dance of constantly speeding up, slowing down, braking, and idling. In urban areas particularly, the faster the speed limit or the feel of the street, the more starting and stopping drivers do. When traffic speeds slow down overall, the flow becomes smoother, and the result is less pollution. Lower speed limits have also been found to reduce emissions at highway speeds.[101]

The best scenario of all when it comes to air pollution has nothing to do with tailpipe filters or hybrid, electric, or zero-emissions car technology. The way to reduce pollution is to reduce driving, plain and simple.

The best proof of this comes during the Olympics. Athletes, like the rest of us, can't do their work well while breathing bad air, but unlike the rest of us their needs are seen as an urgent reason to reduce emissions. During the 1996 games in Atlanta, car travel restrictions resulted in 23% less morning traffic. During that time period, ozone concentrations decreased by 28%, and emergency care visits for asthma went down by 41%.[102] A study of Beijing residents before, during, and after their 2008 Olympics found that their heart health improved significantly during the traffic and industrial restrictions that were part of the $17 billion campaign to clean up the city's air—but risk factors went right back up after the restrictions ended.[103]

The solution to both traffic congestion frustrations and the urgent public health crisis of air pollution is painfully obvious: we have to stop driving. Far from being an impossibility or a dreadful hardship, dramatically reducing the amount we drive is one of the easiest and most cost-effective measures we can take.

The story of the last century has been about choices vacillating, in personal and public investment, between the center and the ever-increasing outskirts. Several waves of suburban migration were fueled by racism masked as concerns about safety and quality of life. But it's becoming increasingly clear that the outskirts were the bum deal, to the detriment of all of us, but especially a burden to those who live there.

Demand is made up of our choices, behaviors, and habits. And this is, in economics-speak, elastic. We change our routines all the time and we like to find new and better ways to do things. And we love choices. If our only alternative option to get to work is a long and uncomfortable bus ride, of course we would rather drive; and if our drive is congested, of course we'll lobby to have the road widened. But if we can have just as nice a trip on a clean, fast commuter train, or if there is a low-traffic bike route all the way from our house to the center city, we'll try out all our options and settle on the combination that works best. Where those other options exist, everyone benefits, people are happier, and the economy thrives.

But in the U.S. it has long been our policy to tackle traffic congestion from the supply side, which is far less elastic and extraordinarily expensive to boot. We build more road capacity, widening congested highways and even city streets, redesigning intersections and interchanges so that car traffic can flow quickly and freely, and building new highways to connect existing ones and bypass the extra snarled areas where people enter and exit.

"We *can* build our way out of congestion!" is the refrain, but this optimistic statement has been proven again and again over the decades to be tragically false.[104]

Here is how it works: Your elected leaders, working together over years or decades, advocate successfully for federal funding for a major road project to help enliven your city's economy. Maybe it's a new bypass or connector, with a couple of new exits. Or maybe the freeway is just widened. Once the project is finished, it's great—the people who were avoiding the old road, because it had too much traffic, decide to use it again. Developers take the opportunity to buy up land and create a new residential neighborhood, and a shopping plaza across the way for good measure. People move into the new houses, others shop or get jobs at the new stores. As a result of this success, the new road doesn't stay empty—after one year or five, it's completely congested again. The people who now rely on the road are frustrated and demand better. Developers, done with their projects, ask for new opportunities. An engineering team at the transportation department starts putting together a funding plan to add a lane. And so it continues.

The widest highway in the world is the Katy Freeway into Houston, Texas, which was expanded in 2008 to a whopping 26 lanes. After the $2.8 billion project was completed, rush hour travel times decreased by a not-insignificant ten or fifteen minutes. The new, smoother freeway attracted new stores and developments along it, and has been hailed as a great success—for now.

The institute that measured the traffic impact of the freeway, however, made a few omissions. The increased traffic on connecting highways and local roads and neighborhood streets was not measured. So we don't know if the ten minutes saved by suburban commuters was counterbalanced by ten extra minutes spent in traffic within the city.

What's more, the same error appears in many official measures of traffic congestion—they forget to take into account that when people are able to drive faster, they choose to drive farther. New users flock to new roads, and everyone who already drove there now feels free to use it even more.

In a nutshell: if you build it, they will come.

The most responsible path in most cases is simply to not build new roads. But the forces advocating for that option are usually not as well-funded or connected as their adversaries. Nobody wants a road construction or widening project in their own back yard, so they tend to be built in the backyards of the people with the least political clout—low-income communities where rates of car ownership are lowest, and for whom a major road serves more as a dividing wall than a way to get anywhere. These are the same urban commuters whose bus commute is likely to increase by ten minutes thanks to the freeway widening that shaves a few minutes from their suburban neighbors' trips.

We take the road-expansion approach to congestion and pollution for a lot of reasons, with misinformation, politics, and profits being no small factors. But why does this approach gain such public support, instead of demand-based approaches that would give us choices that we might like better? Why, by the same token, is it so easy to blame the ills created by clogged traffic on the vehicles that pollute the least, rather than attempting to reduce that traffic?

It makes perfect sense only if you assume that we will always keep driving, and always keep expanding our roads and suburbs outward. It is difficult to imagine this changing, especially since it has been such a major force in our most recent period of prosperity. Our economy, rocky as it is, was built on this foundation of endless outward expansion.

But we are already driving less, not more—by quite a lot. The state of the economy and every demographic trend suggests we will actually continue to drive less and less for quite some time. Since the housing bubble burst, exurban expansion has stalled.[105] The result has been a much needed beginning: a shift in demand. In 2008, Americans drove 3% fewer miles—and traffic congestion dropped 30%. Similar results cost almost three billion dollars to achieve in the evening commute on the Katy Freeway. We can artificially increase the demand for a road with new projects in growing metro areas—but in just as many other places, demand is shrinking.

Few roads have been as contested and for as long as the Embarcadero Freeway that ran along the waterfront of San Francisco.[106]

The Embarcadero was built in 1958 as part of a planned network of ten freeways that would crisscross the city. Residents fought back, and by the end of the decade, seven out of the ten projects had been scrapped. Many never gave up the fight. In 1985, a plan was created to remove it. Funding had been identified, design reviews were passed, and the city council was on board, as well as a broad coalition of groups, including business leaders who hoped to revitalize the waterfront.

But the plan was resoundingly defeated in a ballot measure by voters. Part of their concern was cost, with $171 million needed to remove it and rebuild the area. But the real deal breaker was traffic. Business owners feared they would be cut off from customers, and residents feared that freeway traffic would go straight onto the already-congested city streets where they lived.

Four years later, the Loma Prieta Earthquake changed everything. The Embarcadero Freeway was so badly damaged that it had to be closed. There were two options for moving forward: Rebuild it, either with another double-decker freeway or with a tunnel, or simply remove it.

The question was made easier by the fact that a freeway-removal plan already existed and had broad-based support. Estimates quickly showed that the cost of replacing the freeway by any means was far higher than the bill for tearing it down. What sealed the deal was that everyone could see the traffic results of its removal firsthand. As predicted, city street traffic was snarled immediately after the quake. But that only lasted a few days. People adjusted to their new set of options and traffic rapidly went back to normal.

The freeway was removed and replaced with an arterial road and one of the most glorious public spaces in urban America, a huge park along the waterfront, complete with a wide, well-marked path for cycling, rollerblading, running, and walking.

The removal spurred $300 million in development, created two new residential neighborhoods, brought the once disused Ferry Building back to life.

Lessons learned: When you build a freeway, a lot of people will come drive on it, and to depend on it. But when you build a gorgeous park and create new developable land on a major city's waterfront, people will flock to that, too, and rely on it for similar activities of traveling, shopping, and relaxing—and with more positive consequences for the city.

To go further, there is evidence to show that removing large roads serves traffic flow better than expanding them does. The Embarcadero isn't the only freeway removal project that failed to leave traffic chaos in its wake. Popular movements have been resisting freeways ever since they began to be built in cities. Some of these campaigns have been successful, but in most cases the roads have been built regardless.

One of the best freeway removal success stories is in Seoul, South Korea, a massive freeway through the center of the city was removed in 2005. The Cheonggyecheon River, which it had covered over, was restored and the area around it became a public park. Critics predicted gridlock after the loss of a road that had carried 168,000 cars a day. Instead, traffic times around the city improved, as did air quality and business revenues in the vicinity of the new park.[107]

In the U.S., freeways have rarely been removed unless they are damaged beyond repair, and even then they are usually replaced at great cost. But decreases in traffic are starting to achieve what earthquakes and activists haven't—in recent years, both Baltimore and New Haven have demolished pieces of their poorly connected and little used "freeways to nowhere," though neither has managed to knit the minority communities on either side back together again.

Expanding roads does not prevent congestion; but by some measures, traffic congestion is not actually a bad thing. A failing economy, after all, improves the flow of traffic immeasurably—the empty streets of Detroit are a case in point. Our economy is built on easy and cheap access to cars, gas, and roads, and when people are clamoring to use these it generally means that we are staying afloat, if not thriving. Americans' reduced amount of driving is almost certainly the result of a bad economy. But recent research has honed in on the local level and found that when we drive less, local economies do not suffer as a result.[108] This study confirms the causality—being better off leads us to drive more, not the other way around. But it also confirms what business owners along bike lanes are starting to figure out: not all roads to prosperity must be filled with bumper to bumper traffic.

To effectively and affordably tackle the problem of air pollution, we need to stop building new roads and burn less fuel. It's as simple as that. To achieve that, we need to drive less, we need shorter distances between the places we go, and we need thriving local economies that provide a lot of options. Traffic congestion will never go away as long as there are still cars on the road; but in order to escape its worst effects we must begin to see it as the least of our concerns.

The bicycle is no silver bullet, but it is an instrument that is proven unusually effective in all of these things. The only infrastructure investments that make sense in our new economic climate are ones that reduce demand for driving and induce demand for bicycling. The easier and more intuitive it is to use our public streets on a bicycle, the more people will do it, and the easier it will be for all of us to get where we are going . . . and to breathe.

Parking

I used to take great pride in my parking skills. The only off-limits places to lock my bike were handrails; any other stationary object was fair game. Six bikes deep and three high on a "no parking" street sign? No problem. Hanging from a chain link fence? Better take a photo. The loop on the handle of an empty newspaper box? Turns out it's exactly the right size to thread my u-lock through, if I don't mind my bike rearing up at a sharp angle. When all else failed, there was the most creative and socially perilous option of all—asking a stranger if you could lock up together.

It's been a while since I had any reason for such parking creativity here in Portland. The reason is the proliferation of the bike corral.

The bike corral is a simple idea. You take on-street parking spaces and put a row of bike parking staples in them. The lead-up is controversial, but the transformation is magical, every business owner's dream: instead of places for two paying customers to park outside your front door, you have room for two dozen.

By 2006, the number of people biking around Portland, Oregon was rising dramatically every year, and there just wasn't enough parking. People would lock to anything in sight. On some blocks, you could barely walk down the street for all the parked bikes. Business owners were fed up.

The city began experimenting with bike corrals, one or two a year, awkwardly designed and surrounded by curbs or bollards that made them hard to use. Clunky as they were, the corrals were always full. So in fall, 2008, the city rolled out a new, simplified, cheaper bike corral design, along with a press release laying out the case for them. Bike corrals keep sidewalks clear, the city's transportation bureau argued, they improve traffic safety through better sight lines, improve retail business, and are more cost-effective per square foot than providing free car parking.[109]

The announcement went over like a ton of bricks. The city was wasting its money and making itself a laughingstock, critics grumbled, by taking such dramatic measures to cater to a fringe minority of cyclists.

The first corrals were installed in front of prominent local businesses that were excited to have them. Instantly, the grumbling stopped and the wait list began to grow. Bicycling customers voted with their wallets, and business owners quickly observed that a quadrupling or more of customer parking capacity is nothing to sneeze at. At the beginning of 2011, there were more than 60 corrals, with a waiting list two years long. As of April, 2013, Portland has 97 bike corrals and a long waiting list remains.[110]

> *"Minimum parking requirements act like a fertility drug for cars."*
> —Donald Shoup

An astonishing amount of space in most urban cores is dedicated to the publicly-subsidized storage of private property. But parking is not just about vehicle storage—it's about the shape and character of a community. It's about what public space is used for, who has access to it, and who pays.

Parking and roads go hand in hand. One cannot exist without the other. Together, they take up a stupendous amount of space. By one calculation, 43,000 square miles of land in the U.S. are paved—an area the size of the state of Ohio.[111] Most of this pavement is clustered in urban areas, and includes streets, parking lots, and driveways—or "habitat for cars" as scientists sometimes call it.

Some cities provide more automotive habitat than others. Streets alone occupy 40% of the land in downtown Houston—when you include parking, 65% of the city is covered with asphalt. In Little Rock, 61% of the city is paved; in Milwaukee it's 54%.[112] In Salt Lake City, 65% of the downtown area and over 30% of the land area in residential neighborhoods is paved over.[113]

These are just a few of the U.S. cities where more than half of useable urban land is devoted primarily to moving and storing private cars. Some of that land is highly valuable—or would be if it were not surrounded by what have been termed "parking craters," huge areas of cities that resemble orderly war zones, featuring only a few buildings in a sea of parking lots. Central and waterfront areas, like the Embarcadero, are proven to be worth hundreds of millions in development investments alone.[114]

Car parking remains a major part of our economy, and it is easy to realize why its availability and low price are clung to so fiercely. Parking allows access for customers to stores, employees to work, entrepreneurs to meetings, tourists to places where they can deposit all their money, the needy to services, residents to their homes. Because of this, it's harder to see that the costs are so high that they outweigh all economic benefits provided.

Covering our cities with asphalt isn't just ugly; it eats up millions of dollars in taxable land revenue per year. Highways and parking lots represent a massive amount of taxable property that could yield thousands of dollars per lot, per year—representing millions of dollars of lost revenue for cities. Instead, the constant need for maintenance drains public and private coffers—and this cost is overshadowed by the opportunity cost of what could be built in our cities instead.

Yet all this space is given away freely as a standard practice. In the US, 99% of trips by car end up in a free spot.[115] The value of that land—and to a lesser extent, the costs of paving, sweeping, policing, and maintaining it—makes parking one of the largest subsidies going. Donald Shoup, the world's foremost expert on all things parking, calculates that the average parking subsidy to a U.S. commuter who drives to work is $5 per work day. Shoup estimated the entire parking subsidy of free parking to be at least $127 billion in 2002—an amount that would put a nice dent in the cash-strapped transportation budget.[116]

We are quite literally paying people to drive.

It's not just taxpayers footing the bill, but businesses and housing developers. This is not always because they see it as a good investment. In fact, it's prohibitive—the average cost to build structured parking in the U.S. is $15,000 per space. But most cities have had parking minimum laws on the books since the 1950s, requiring any new housing, workplaces, and commercial developments to provide a certain number of parking spaces whether or not their residents, employees, or customers drive. There is always some pushback against these requirements, partly as a matter of space and subsidy, and the huge costs involved.[117]

Induced demand is just as much a factor in parking as it is in traffic congestion. The more car parking spaces we build, the more people choose to drive, increasing the demand for yet more parking. Shoup's prescription for cities with major parking woes is something like congestion pricing: make parking more expensive. He suggests pricing parking so that there is always one spot open on every city block. This results in fewer people circling for parking, thus reducing congestion and emissions. It ensures higher turnover of parking spaces and thus better retail sales. And it opens the door for cities where the general population is not subsidizing the wealthiest residents, especially in cities like Washington, DC or Baltimore where nearly half of residents do not own cars.

In 2010, Jesse McCann was looking for a building to open a bar in Portland, Oregon. Like many a business owner, he was thrilled when he finally found one with a big parking lot right out front with room for five cars. But instead of using the lot to provide car parking for his customers, he fenced it off and filled the space with outdoor seating and a rack for 63 bicycles. People thought he was crazy. But McCann's investment paid off—from the day Apex Bar opened, its outdoor tables and bike racks have been full to overflowing on nice days.

Business owners tend to like bike parking. Many are wary at first, especially when car parking spaces are being replaced. But once a bike corral or staple is put in, the value added becomes immediately clear, and as they become more common, they are more broadly accepted and welcomed.

Bike parking is undeniably an affordable investment. For each vehicle, bike parking takes up ten times less space than car parking and the cost is from 30 to 300 times less.[118] When bike parking is available at destinations, people are more likely to choose to ride to those places, and also to ride overall.[119]

A study in Melbourne, Australia found that bike parking brought in five times the revenue of car parking.[120] A study in Toronto found that customers who biked and walked to local businesses spent more money overall than those who drove.[121] Critics of bike corrals often voice the concern that the city will lose revenue from parking meters. But parking is so undervalued that meters typically charge less than the value of a parking space; it makes more sense to maximize capacity—and the benefits.

The bicycle parking boom is taking many creative forms. "Bike Stations" or "Bike Hubs" at transit centers or in office districts charge bike commuters a small monthly fee for the use of showers, secure bike parking, and a bike shop and repair station. Whimsical bike racks designed by artists (David Byrne created a series for New York) are embraced by commercial districts for their distinctive style. Churches and schools are installing bike racks on an "if you build it, they will come" basis, and it's working. Bicycle parking all over the country is stepping out from next to the dumpster behind the restaurant and taking its proud place right next to the front door. And the economy is reaping the benefits.

Bicycle parking brings all of the same benefits as car parking and has others as well. By inducing more people to ride bicycles, it contributes to better health, less poverty, safer streets, more breathable air—and perhaps of most direct financial value, it reduces congestion and frees up car parking. It does cost money to provide bike parking for free—but this cost is so low in relation to the benefits, that the city would profit even if it paid everyone five bucks a pop to park their bikes.

Converting car parking to bike parking is one of the cheapest, easiest, and most effective ways for any city to make a sizeable dent in the bad economics of our current transportation system.

But the law of induced demand cannot be escaped. One of the problems bike-friendly cities face is overcrowding of bike parking areas. Bike parking in Amsterdam is so freely available that many people own multiple bikes and keep them parked at transit centers around the city to ride when they happen to be in the neighborhood. The benefits must outweigh the costs of dealing with this bike jam, or the business-minded local government would doubtless begin charging for parking.

It's a problem I hope we all have the pleasure of dealing with at some time in the near future.

Rethinking Safety

8

June, 2013—The Wall Street Journal released an interview with editorial board member Dorothy Rabinowitz. The video is a short news-format segment titled "Death by Bicycle," in which Rabinowitz discusses her opinions about the CitiBike, New York City's bike-share system that had launched barely a week prior.

The bike-share docking stations, she tells an earnestly nodding reporter, have "begrimed" some of Manhattan's finest neighborhoods. Bike-share, she declaims, has been imposed upon a reluctant majority of New Yorkers by a totalitarian government at the behest of an all-powerful bike lobby. She also shares her candid thoughts on bicycle safety:

"Before this, every citizen knew—who was in any way sentient—that the most important danger in the city is not the yellow cabs. It's the bicyclists who veer in and out of the sidewalk, empowered by the city administration, with the idea that they are privileged, because they are helping, part of all the good, forward-looking things."

The interview immediately went viral, and Rabinowitz soon reprised her role in a second faux news segment, doubling down with a smile.

Rabinowitz is far from the only person to believe that bicyclists are a threat to safety on city streets. The rebuttal to her concern, however, came shortly afterwards, in a report on CitiBike's first month. The bright blue short-term rental bicycles had been checked out for 500,000 rides in the first month. They had been ridden for a total of over a million miles. Only three crashes were reported, each resulting in injuries to the rider—in two cases minor, and one serious after a van driver ran a red light.[122]

By the most conservative estimate, that data means that bike-share users—many of whom are new to city cycling, and are unlikely to wear helmets—are two and a half times less likely to be involved in a crash[123] than someone riding their own bicycle[124]—and much less likely than a yellow cab.[125]

Nobody's sure why, but bike-share systems enjoy a particularly good safety record. In general, though, whatever bicycle you're using, traveling by bike is safer than driving by almost any measure.

The best thing for bike safety though, hands down, is more people out on the road riding bikes.

The bicycling rate in the U.S. is rising quickly [126]—and you might reasonably think that the rate of crashes would at least proportionately rise with it as everyone from wobbly novice riders to the outright safety-averse take to the roads.

In reality, as ridership goes up, crash rates stay flat or go down.

The phenomenon, dubbed "safety in numbers," was first identified in 2003 by public health researcher Peter Jacobsen.[127] Officials in Pasadena, California asked him to evaluate if their city "was a dangerous place to bicycle." Unsure how to approach the question, Jacobsen began looking at crash data from various communities where bicycle ridership had fluctuated over time.

What he found surprised him: The number of crashes involving bikes correlated with the number of riders in a community. As ridership fluctuated, so did the crash rate. More riders, fewer crashes; fewer riders, more crashes.

This happened too abruptly to be caused by slow-moving factors like infrastructure development and cultural change. Bicycling becomes safer when the number of riders increases, Jacobsen concluded, at least in part *because* the number of riders increases.

The inverse happens, as well. One data set Jacobsen looked at covered 49 years of biking history in the United Kingdom. Those numbers showed that cycling became safer during the oil crisis of the 1970s, when more people started biking. Once the crisis ended, both ridership and safety dropped.

Safety in numbers has been studied quite a bit, in part because it is so counterintuitive. Case studies around the world continue to prove it to be correct.[128]

In recent years, something even more surprising has been showing up in research: when there are more people bicycling on the roads, everyone becomes safer—not just people on bicycles, but people walking and driving as well.[129]

The safety in numbers effect works, explains Jacobsen, because when there are a lot of people bicycling, people who drive cars take notice. And they learn. They become more attentive, slow down, pass more cautiously, double-check their blind spots, expect the unexpected. They sense that the road has become a more complicated place, and adjust their behavior accordingly. As a result, they drive more safely and everyone benefits—not least the drivers themselves.

Building up a critical mass of cyclists doesn't happen in a vaccuum though. You can achieve a temporary safety in numbers effect when a large group of people bike together through streets that would be uncomfortable and feel dangerous alone. But to get that effect to stick around for the long term you need to attract more riders by making changes on the street itself.

Bicycle infrastructure makes bicycling safer by two measures: First, by making bicycling a more attractive, convenient, and comfortable choice. Second, by providing clarity and often physical protection to reduce the chances of a car and bike colliding.

Studies consistently show that small safety improvements attract a large numbers of cyclists. Certainly, people who live in neighborhoods that have a lot of bicycle infrastructure bicycle more—enjoying the safety in numbers effect as well as the protection of the infrastructure.[130]

Good bike streets don't always have bike lanes or concrete barriers. Every type of street has its own needs. Quiet residential streets without bike-specific embellishments are safer than bike lanes on busy streets—though they are not always faster and they do not always take you where you need to go. The busier the street, the greater the intervention required to make it comfortable to bicycle on and safer for all users.[131]

The majority of bicycle crashes happen on streets designed with no thought for cycling.[132] By the same token, protected bike lanes, of the sort being exemplified by Chicago and New York and increasingly taken up by cities like Lincoln, Nebraska as good investments on their busiest streets, can reduce risk of injuries in all crashes by up to ninety percent.[133]

In 2010, Manhattan Borough President Scott Stringer had heard a lot of complaints about lawbreaking among cyclists. So he sent staff out to observe what happened on eleven different streets as neutrally as possible, keeping track of every incident they witnessed that occurred in those streets' bike lanes.

They observed 1,700 instances of traffic infractions being committed. They counted 741—more than a third of the incidents—counts of people on foot standing or walking in the bike lanes, including one collision between someone cycling and someone stepping into the lane. In 353 of the incidents, the bike lane was blocked outright, primarily by a motor vehicle—18% of these were taxis and limos, and 13% were city vehicles. In one instance, a school bus idled in the bike lane for seven minutes. Several cases were recorded of "unmarked Police vehicles in apparent non-emergency situations cutting through protected bike lanes." 77 near-dooring incidents were counted, in which people opened car doors into the bike lane, causing someone on a bike to swerve out of the way into oncoming traffic.

Meanwhile, 242 cyclists were observed riding the wrong way in the bike lane (during a two hour period on one block there was more wrong way bike traffic than otherwise), and 237 rode through a red light.

Stringer's study recommended not cracking down on cyclists, but creating infrastructure that better serves their needs. When your two choices, he pointed out, are to take a street the wrong way for a block or travel eight long blocks out of your way and cross several intersections where cyclists are often hit, what would you do?

From a civic perspective, it's cheaper and easier to restripe the wrong way street to add a two-way bike lane than it is to throw your limited resources into cracking down on people who have no good choices.

Infrastructure is safer—and more effective at producing orderly behavior—than traffic enforcement. Enforcement can have a chilling effect on bicycling.

In 2015, the *Tampa Bay Times* investigated tickets written by local police for bicycle infractions. "Police say they are gung ho about bike safety and focused on stopping a plague of bike thefts," wrote the reporters. "But here's something they don't mention about the people they ticket: Eight out of 10 are black." They go on to describe a litany of fines given for questionable violations such as walking a bicycle without a light or not having a receipt to prove ownership of the bicycle or something carried on it. Moreover, they found, police were targeting particularly high-crime neighborhoods, with the assumption that cyclists were more likely to be criminals; but only 20% of the adults ticketed were arrested, some for carrying small amounts of drugs and others for things like refusing to sign a ticket. Some individuals were stopped over a dozen times, and one person was stopped three times in a single day. [134] When the article came out, other stories of police harassment for biking while black or brown emerged from around the country. The penalty of a police stop isn't just a ticket, though those can be costly—there's also the embarrassment, not to mention the sense of unsafety. And the impact on civic life is absolutely chilling.

Cyclists' reputation as consummate lawbreakers only seems to hold true in places where the streets don't adequately support bicycling.

At intersection counts in cities throughout Oregon, two of which—Corvallis and Eugene—are among the most bicycle-friendly places in the nation, 94% of people on bicycles stopped at red lights, a far cry from the scofflaw mythology. It is six times more common to drive a car over the speed limit on neighborhood streets.[134B] It turns out that when people on bicycles are treated seriously as traffic, they act accordingly. Studies in Chicago before and after new bicycle signals were put in found that cyclist compliance at red lights tripled, from 31% to 81%.

The most frequent bicycle offense that leads to a crash is riding on the wrong side of the road, against traffic—where nobody in a car expects to see you, especially when turning onto the road.[135]

But wrong-way riding is not done out of arrogance, disrespect, or reckless abandon. Many of us learned as children, and kids are still taught to this day, that this is the only safe way to ride. That's tragically false—it is, in fact, one of the most dangerous things you can do while bicycling. The fact that so many still believe otherwise represents a major gap in bicycle advocacy—and a huge opportunity for outreach.

On occasions when I ride my bicycle around town without a helmet, I hear about it.

When I go downtown, people will take it on themselves to berate my helmetless state, sometimes from blocks away. Once, an acquaintance swerved his pickup truck uncomfortably close so he could lean out the window and tell me to put a helmet on. Often, it's children who want to let me know that I am not safe.

And no wonder. Bicycle safety has, for many decades, been equated with bicycle helmets.

The efficacy of helmets is not in question for protecting the head against injury to a limited extent. But just how much protection is given is currently under considerable debate.[136]

To some, helmets are everything important in bicycle advocacy—a matter of personal responsibility, and a realistic acknowledgment of what can go wrong. To others, helmets are a distraction from the factors that protect us against crashes in the first place. Moreover, to focus on helmets as the epitome of bicycle safety is a subtle way of suggesting that bicycling is an unusually dangerous activity and that it's up to us if we get hurt.

One thing we do know is that mandatory helmet laws not only do not increase cycling safety, but may reduce safety overall. This is through the Safety in Numbers mechanism. Helmet laws have been shown to actively dissuade people from riding bicycles, though whether it is because of the inconvenience of a helmet or the tacit assumption that cycling is dangerous I do not know. But clearly mandating or overly focusing on bicycle helmets is a barrier for bicycling, increasing the cost of entry quite literally and putting the unlikely risks in our minds rather than the manifest daily benefits.

We also know that in the safest countries for bicycling, nobody wears a bicycle helmet, unless they are embarking on an athletic ride hunched over a road bike. And perhaps that is why countries like Canada, Australia, and the U.S. are so hung up on helmets—they are a part of the aesthetic and cultural apparatus of riding a bicycle as a sport, which is still largely how bikes are seen here.

Whatever the key to bicycle safety is, it does not lie in helmets or any other protective gear—it is in the shape, speed, and use of our roads. The Netherlands sees a quarter of all its travel done by bicycle, and 85% of its residents ride a bike at least once a week—and a good deal of the rest of their trips are done on transit and on foot. This is the result of a consistent approach to providing safe places to ride; but both the infrastructure and the safety are also a function of the sheer number of riders.

It's a snowball effect. When bicycling becomes safer, more people ride. And when more people ride, bicycling becomes even safer.

But perhaps when we focus on risk and crashes, we are looking at traffic safety all wrong.

When you calculate the risk of being in a serious crash in relation to the number of miles you travel, your risk while bicycling is a bit higher, though not as high as that of walking. When you calculate it differently, based on the number of hours you spend on the road either pedaling or driving, your chances of survival are about the same.

In the bigger picture, though, bicycling is safer than driving. Much safer. Choosing to bicycle makes the world safer for the people around you, for one thing. Many of the advances in automotive safety over the last century have been focused on protecting cars' occupants at ever-increasing speeds. But often these so-called safety improvements, like increased vehicle size and weight, are profoundly dangerous for bystanders, bicyclists, and people in smaller and lighter cars. If you're on a bike, by contrast, your chances of seriously injuring someone else are nearly zero.

If you expand your definition of safety to include living a long and healthy life, there's simply no comparison. Bicycling, even a little, is so good for your health on so many levels that the benefits greatly overshadow the risks.

The canonical study on the topic looked at all the risks and benefits of cycling, and found that, at the end of the day, the benefits win big. The benefits of more physical activity outweigh the risks of crashes and breathing in car exhaust by a ratio of nine to one. The result: switching from driving to cycling increases your average life expectancy by seven months.

That study is from the Netherlands, where your risks on a bike are quite low. So I went looking for more studies from less bike-friendly places and was surprised to find that the Dutch had come up with the most conservative estimate. Other studies, using similar criteria—though some took into account the increased lifespan of everyone in an area due to reduced air pollution from more people bicycling—had the benefits of bicycling outweighing the risks by as much as 96 to 1.[137]

•   •   •

Safety, like traffic congestion, is a concept that often leads us in counterproductive directions.

What does it mean to be safe? Most people, when asked why they do not bicycle more, cite safety—cycling often seems too dangerous to contemplate, especially from a windshield perspective. Beyond this, there is widespread myth, which Rabinowitz puts words to most clearly, that everyone who rides a bicycle does so recklessly, endangering themselves and others and setting our whole orderly system of rules and norms on its head.

Rabinowitz's misperceptions are shared by many. You don't need to go far to find statements that bicyclists all run red lights, or frequently kill pedestrians. If you go a bit farther, the data shows both these claims are greatly overstated.[138]

Collisions between people bicycling and walking are rare; serious injuries and fatalities are even more infrequent; such tragedies occur less than once in a year in New York City; in that same city, a person on foot is killed by a car nearly every other day.[139] In crashes that occur between a bike and a car, the driver is found to be at fault 50-90% of the time; these crashes are far more likely to occur on streets that do not provide safe infrastructure.

But data does not go very far when it comes to what we feel is safe. Many of our most ingrained ideas about safety run entirely counter to the facts, even when those facts are widely publicized. As many as a third of U.S. adults fear flying, despite the extremely low chance of being injured in an airplane crash. The reality, that you are far more likely to be injured in a car on the way to the airport, is such common knowledge as to be joked about. By a similar token, when I was growing up, inner cities were seen as dangerous places, wracked by gun violence; but your chances of being injured or killed by a car in the suburbs were far higher than being caught in gunfire downtown. Yet we still fear what we fear, and the reasons for that, when examined, are not always very nice to reflect upon.

We have a very large cultural blind spot when it comes to cars. Using the roads by any means is one of the most dangerous things you will do on a daily basis; in a car, you are not very much less at risk, but you become a tremendous danger to others.

Yet crashes are so commonplace that even when they affect us directly, we see them as flukes rather than a real and systemic threat. We call them "accidents" and think of them as inevitable yet unlikely to happen to us. The legal system treats them the same way; unless a driver who causes a fatal crash was drunk or leaves the scene, criminal penalties are low or nonexistent. Texting and talking on the phone while driving are the functional equivalents to driving while drunk, yet the acts are so commonplace that it is difficult to either pass or enforce laws against them.

In the 1920s, when cars and their drivers were feared and demonized, this perception was backed up by the high rate of fatal crashes.

Cycling today seems to have captured our imagination in somewhat the same way, but without the actual threat. And experience is proving to mollify anxious critics. Within six weeks, the same reporters that had forecast doom for CitiBike found themselves trying the system out and changing their minds entirely.

•   •   •

"It was on the last day of October that the accident occurred. Pollyanna, hurrying home from school, crossed the road at an apparently safe distance in front of a swiftly approaching motor car. Just what happened, no one could seem to tell afterward. Neither was there any one found who could tell why it happened or who was to blame that it did happen." —Pollyanna, Eleanor H. Porter, 1913

One third of us are likely to be in a serious car crash at some point in our lives. Car crashes are the number one cause of death for people in the U.S. under age 25.[140] At 26 and older, your odds of dying in a car crash do not go down very much—in fact, if you are still driving in your eighties you are nearly as high a risk behind the wheel as when you were a teenager. Past your mid-thirties, your risk of cancer and heart disease become much higher than any other threat, but this is also to the point—these are sedentary diseases. Of the top ten causes of death in the U.S., seven are affected by our exposure to and reliance on cars.[141]

If you cannot afford a car, and you do not live in a place where other options are safe and convenient, then you are out of luck. You are more likely to be hit by a car when you leave your house; you are less likely to go out unnecessarily, putting you at greater risk of sedentary diseases. If you live in poverty with no car, you are less likely to have good access to a grocery store, which increases those risks yet further. You are certainly more likely to be disabled from any of these causes, and less likely to have access to adequate health care or to be able to find or keep work. All of these things cost money, which you are, of course, less likely to be able to pay.[142]

The economic impact of the things we do in the name of traffic safety is nothing less than devastating for society. Traffic crashes are increasingly recognized as a worldwide epidemic.[143] In the U.S. alone, over 34,000 people die in traffic crashes each year and over 2 million are injured.[144] Nearly 300,000 of these injured people suffer permanently disabling injuries each year.[145] These injuries often mean that you are no longer able to drive; to add insult, they just as often also mean that you cannot get around without use of a car, and are often no longer able to work. Instead, people with incapacitating injuries—and a number of other non-car-related disabilities—must rely for economic survival on family members, social safety nets, and an insurance and legal system—all of which occupy shaky ground in these times.

Estimates of the societal costs of car crashes vary. One reckoning takes into account the medical costs directly related to crashes as well as the work lost, and comes up with a cost of nearly $100 billion, or $500 per licensed driver, each year.[146] Other accounts go further. A 2011 study by the AAA included a broader range of costs, from legal bills to lost ability to do unpaid household labor to quality of life, property damage, emergency response, and traffic delays that result from crashes. Their estimated cost was much higher—$3 billion a year, or more than three times their estimated cost of congestion.[147] That's $1,500 per person, per year. The costs of crashes exceed congestion, the AAA found, in every urban metropolitan area studied.

A federal study of the cost of car crashes in 2000 that included property damage and travel delays due to crashes, came up with an even higher figure: $230 billion. Of that amount, $33 billion was spent on medical costs—for perspective, that's the same amount as that year's federal highway budget.

One afternoon, waiting for friends at a coffeeshop, I picked up a book someone had left behind—a guide to helping aging parents adjust to life without a car. The author offered strategies for adult children on time management and setting boundaries with their parent's transportation demands. The book provided scripts for that anxious moment when you finally confiscate your aging parent's keys, and advised calling the police if the parent insisted on driving anyway. When newly shut-in people were upset, the author counseled therapy.

I searched the book in vain for any mention of ways that a person who was too old to drive could possibly have any kind of self-sufficient life. Perhaps if they relocated to a neighborhood where they could have easy access to stores and social destinations on foot or in a wheelchair? No mention. What if they could ride the bus? Nope. How about a bicycle or recumbent trike as a way to go out and be active? Not a chance.

The book left me queasy and shaken and understanding a bit better why people opt to move to retirement homes rather than living "independently" in trapped isolation. It's all too easy to place the full responsibility for traffic safety on the actions of individuals; but it's easier to forget what unforgiving limits the built environment can set on those actions.

In a car-oriented world, old age becomes a disability for many, long before it might in a more walkable neighborhood. The more car-reliant your daily life is, the lower the threshold becomes for frailness, injury, or failing eyesight to be experienced as outright disabling—and dangerous to other road users.[148]

In the next twenty years, the number of elderly people with drivers licenses in the U.S. is expected to triple. Many in the baby boomer generation who were of the demographic that populated the suburbs are already opting to move back to the urban areas they fled as young professionals. As our population ages, the demand for real, safe, convenient alternatives to driving is only going to become more apparent, and expensive stop gap measures like transit shuttles are going to become less and less effective.

The very young suffer as much in a car-oriented world as the very old. The history of our health is closely tied with the story and pace of sprawl development, and that is showing most clearly in younger generations. In the 1970s, at least half of kids walked or biked to school; today it is less than 15%,[149] in part because the world has grown more spread out. Families are living farther away from their childrens' schools at the same time as neighborhood schools are closing and consolidating in the face of budget cuts.

The tragedy is that in many areas, walking and bicycling really is unsafe for children. This is not because of the danger of kidnapping, which has always been quite low, but because of the danger of crossing the street. In wealthier areas, parents drive their kids to school. In less well off areas, kids must rely on the bus. But as budgets tighten, often school bus service is the first to go. In Akron, Ohio, schoolbuses no longer serve students who live less than two miles from their school. In a recent month, eight kids were struck by cars while walking to school, with children from poor or predominantly African American neighborhoods being most at risk.[150] It is rare but not unheard of for Child Protective Services to investigate parents in low-income neighborhoods for allowing their children to walk or bicycle to school.

In some school districts, in the name of safety, children are not allowed to walk or bike to school.[151] At other times of day, general outdoor play and self-powered transportation are greatly curtailed, and this is frequently due to safety concerns as well. The streets used to be children's realm to run, play, and socialize. As recently as the mid-1980s, I and other neighborhood kids walked nearly a mile to school without adults and had free rein over a relatively large territory. But things were already changing then, and nowadays children are much more likely to play indoors. One distressing study showed that nearly 23% of U.S. kids between age 9 and 13 don't engage in any physical activity at all during their free time.[152] Nearly 20% of kids are at high risk for heart disease and diabetes.[153] Inactivity is a self-reinforcing bad habit. Children who are physically active are likely to carry that practice on to adulthood; inactive children likewise.

Kids are the canaries—their declining health and happiness have been reliable early warning signals for anyone who cares to take heed of the scope of the maladies of the general population. Likewise, the sight of children and families riding bicycles on public roads is considered an indicator of the health of a community and its actual bikeability.

The consequences are real. When kids are active enough—and bicycling and walking to school is a good predictor of this, as well as a means towards it—they are healthier, and are more likely to become healthy adults.[154] They are at less risk for diabetes, they have better heart health, they breathe easier, and they are stronger and more flexible. They fall asleep faster at night. They do better at math and reading and have more focus at school, setting them up for better success and health in later life.[155] They are less likely to smoke, they watch less television,[156] and they both know and enjoy their neighborhood better.[157] Among kids who are already overweight, if they exercise regularly, they have better self-esteem and are less likely to be depressed.

Children are also at the greatest risk from car crashes, and have been since the automobile entered the scene. Today, motor vehicle crashes are the leading cause of death for children above age two. At the beginning of the motor age in the U.S., cars were relatively few, but the toll was yet higher. The new epidemic of traffic deaths of children was considered by popular opinion to literally amount to murder. Motorists who killed children were lynched by mobs. Bereft parents protested furiously against this new "juggernaut" or death machine and demanded that speed governors be installed in all cars. Statues were erected in memory of the young victims.

But by the 1930s, the tide turned. Children themselves were assigned the responsibility of staying out of traffic, not jaywalking, and not playing in the street. Beginning at that time, when a child was hurt or killed in a car crash, the child's reckless behavior or the parents' inattention were considered to be the cause, and childrens' deaths in traffic came to be seen as tragic but inevitable. It is sad to contemplate what a grieving mother turned anti-car activist in 1920 would think upon seeing our world today.[158]

Kids and cars are simply not compatible, it seems. Education—such as the "stop, look, and listen" routine drilled into every school child's head—seems to have only a very minor impact on traffic safety for children. Until we are around twelve, our brains are not developed enough to safely handle what adults see as basic traffic situations.[159] Cognitive tasks that kids cannot do well at a young age include perceiving the direction of traffic, estimating the speed of oncoming traffic, and visually checking the environment for oncoming cars.

By the time we are teenagers, we have developed the abilities needed to cross the street safely, but most of us do not have the self control needed to safely drive a car. As with young children, this has more to do with brain development than with character.[160]

The effect on driving behavior and road safety—for teen drivers, their passengers, and others on the road—is manifest. People in this high risk group make up 14% of the U.S. population, but are involved in 30% of the crashes that lead to injury or death.[161] Teen drivers are more dangerous even than drivers in their eighties. And safety education, including showing teens gory movies of car crashes, has little effect.

But we are in a bind. Do we isolate teens, preventing them from independent mobility and accessing jobs, or do we allow them to do something which they are unable to do safely, and consider the tragic effects to be inevitable?

We might ask the same question on our own behalf at any age. Is it truly safe to live in a world that keeps us bound to our houses and cars, and leaves us few options beyond them?

To be effective, efforts to improve traffic safety must rethink what safety means, and for whom. On a government level, this change can have profound implications.

Traffic safety in the U.S. is currently managed on a cost-benefit model that is oriented towards speedy car travel. Roads and intersections receive grades based on how quickly and smoothly cars are able to travel through them. The conditions that improve a road's rankings, though—like wide, curving intersections, lots of lanes, trees and buildings far back from the curb to improve sight lines, and high average speeds—are the exact things that make a road more dangerous as well as uncomfortable to bicycle down or to cross on foot. Often these are the same treatments that induce more congestion, turning local roads into highways that cannot be expanded fast enough to keep up with growing demand.

When many crashes happen on a road, there is an equation for taking that into account as well: the value of each life lost is weighed against the cost of improvements. As a road grows wider and therefore "safer," pedestrian or bicycle safety measures grow more expensive—instead of a crosswalk, a separate traffic light might be necessary, or eventually, when things have gotten really terrible, a costly and unsatisfactory pedestrian bridge over the road.

Economically speaking, to each of us individually, our own life, and the lives of our loved ones, have infinite value—that is to say, there is no amount of money for which we would exchange them. But every department of the federal government must assign a dollar value to a human life, for the purpose of cost-benefit analysis. The federal transportation department estimates the economic impact of each life lost on the roads at $7 million—aside from the direct cost of the crash and emergency response, there's the value each of us puts into the economy through our labor over the years, and that is lost through a traffic death.

When a road or intersection is deemed unsafe, investment is determined in part by looking at the value of the number of fatalities, multiplied by $7 million dollars—and comparing that with the amount it would cost to fix it. All too often, even when we have the right ideas about safe infrastructure, they just don't pencil out.

Consider a more humane way to think about traffic safety: Vision Zero, a Swedish policy that was implemented in 1997, with a goal of achieving zero annual traffic fatalities by 2020. The core principle is that "life cannot be exchanged for other benefits in society." Mobility cannot be exchanged for safety, as we do in our cost-benefit based system in the U.S.

The program calls for a combination of safe infrastructure, safe car design, and strict enforcements of seatbelts. It is particularly focused on controlling speed of travel to the level that maximizes survival. For instance, if there is any chance of conflict between vehicles and pedestrians, then the maximum speed allowed is 30 km/hour—the top speed at which a collision is unlikely to cause life-threatening injuries to the pedestrian.

Sweden has not been entirely successful, but by 2009, they had achieved a 34% reduction in traffic fatalities, and set a new goal of 2050 for reaching zero. Similar policies have been adopted in the UK and in the Netherlands.

This is an alternative to the cost-benefit analysis method currently in use in the United States. Vision Zero and policies like it in effect put an infinite value on human lives, just as we do on our own; this equation trumps all other considerations except those of public health impacts.

Since 2013, the concept of Vision Zero has gained significant currency in the U.S., and several cities have adopted it as a policy. Criticisms have arisen as well, particularly of the increase of law enforcement that tend to be politically attractive as such programs are implemented. In a country where police stops are often informed by racial profiling, increased traffic enforcement is not a universal good.

To truly follow this approach—and to be able to foot the bill—would require a far greater investment than symbolic traffic stops. It needs roads to be scaled down rather than scaled up; for vast roads to be made human size again rather than inadequately bridged with squalid concrete pedestrian overpasses.

When everybody drives, the perceived cost of not driving is too high to be an attractive choice. Big changes are needed all at once in order to break the deadlock—bike-share systems, good bicycle infrastructure that attracts a large number of new riders, slower traffic speeds in every neighborhood, and more human-scale areas that can be navigated without a car would be a good place to start.

Can we afford to implement the broad reforms necessary to make our streets safe and comfortable for people of every age and every means? I would argue that we can't afford not to try.

Bike Lanes
on Main
Street

9

Magnolia Street in Fort Worth, Texas's newly hip Near Southside, is the sort of story that urban planners dream of.

In 2008, this retail-, office-, and apartment-lined street was re-striped. The street had been two lanes in each direction, both of which had been mainly used by cars, plus a few fast and fearless cyclists. In its new incarnation it still had four lanes, one in each direction for cars, and one for bicycles. "It was the first 'road diet' of its kind in Fort Worth, and has been a genuine success," Kevin Buchanan, a local musician and author of the Fort Worthology blog, told me.[162]

The best measure of this success was in the bottom line: after the road was rearranged, restaurant revenues along the street went up a combined total of 179%.

"Not to imply causality," Buchanan added, "but clearly removing car lanes and replacing them with bike lanes had no ill effects on businesses, and of course it can be argued that the safer, slower street and better cycling/walking environment helped business."

The effort to revitalize the street included adding lots of new parking. A 320 space car parking garage went up in the heart of the district; shortly afterward, bicycle parking staples were bolted into the concrete in front of every business, providing spaces for 160 bikes.

The total cost for the parking garage was over 5 million dollars. The total for buying and installing all the bicycle parking came to just over $12,000—less than the cost of a single space in the garage.

On the spring weekend I visited Magnolia Street in 2012, the garage was nearly empty, but bike staples outside neighborhood restaurants and bars were overflowing. A coffeeshop on the street, needing yet more capacity, had built their own bike corral, a row of bike staples drilled into the public right of way. The new spaces more than doubled the shop's previous parking capacity.

By all measures, these improvements were an excellent investment. So much so that other Fort Worth streets were slated to get the same treatment—replacing car capacity with bicycle capacity both on and off the road.

What does a bike-friendly community actually look like? It certainly does not look like anyone's fantasy of a pedestrian or agricultural past. Distances have become too great, cities are too sprawling, and we are all too deeply invested in lives that are spread out across a landscape that has been designed to suit the automobile. Transit is important, but can only take us so far in this dispersed landscape without massive and costly redevelopment of the built environment that is not always done in a way that proves useful and attractive.

This is the genius of the bicycle. Most bike trips are less than 30 minutes. When people ride to get in shape, they tend to go farther,[163] and people who already commute by bike seem content to ride greater, on average, distances to and from work. But for all of the errands of daily life we want easy transportation. Perhaps this is why, in places where bicycling is common, business density increases—there is demand for clustered retail within neighborhoods. Whatever the reason, this does not just make life more convenient for people who bicycle—it provides more choices and shorter trips for everyone in the neighborhood, however they get around.

Not owning a car means I am free from the burden of buying gas, so the money I might otherwise spend at the pump is mine to dispose of in other ways.[164] Because I live in a central neighborhood and walk nearly everywhere, I'm unlikely to seek bargains at chain stores on the outskirts of town. That extra money stays in the neighborhood, much of it going to locally-owned businesses.

The average trip to the pump costs $30-50, depending on what you're driving.[165] Two thirds of that goes straight to oil companies; over a third of what we spend at the pump leaves the country. Unless you live in Houston or Kuwait, your money has a long way to travel. Even if you live next door to the company's headquarters and own stock in it, your economic returns will be slight. These hugely profitable businesses produce relatively few jobs—one job per million dollars of output, compared to twelve times that many in the retail sector.

By contrast, out of every $50 spent in locally owned businesses, $34 stays longer in the local community through taxes, payroll, and local contracts.[166] My own $50 may not make a huge splash, but when most of my neighbors enjoy the same options afforded by bike-friendly streets and thriving local retail, it adds up to something real and measurable.

Economist Joe Cortright calls this effect the "Green Dividend." Portlanders, he finds, drive 20% fewer miles every day than the average resident of a comparable metro area. The total money that we save on those miles we don't drive is $1.1 billion dollars a year. Of this, Cortright estimates that $800 million of this goes right back into our local economy.[167]

That number would be much higher if it included more factors. Driving less allows all Portlanders to enjoy the health benefits of better air quality. And we save a substantial amount of productive time by driving less. Add these factors and our total yearly benefit comes out to $2.6 billion. This is the dividend that we reap for our decent transit system, close-knit neighborhoods, and the relatively tiny investments—amounting to less than one percent of our transportation budget over the past several decades—into bicycle infrastructure.

However small, this infrastructure investment is a key component of the story. If we simply stopped driving but did not have good alternatives, our economy would suffer in much the same way as that of Baltimore, another city with a low-car ownership rates but with depleted populations and much greater poverty levels. Thanks to policies that limit sprawl expansion, combined with decades of slow but steady investments in bikeways instead of freeways, Portlanders have more opportunities than most to travel short distances to grocery stores and restaurants, workplaces and schools. It's a simple thing on its surface, but we reap the benefits, multiplied.

Studies of the effects of bicycling on retail are still coming in, but they produce nearly unanimous results. One fact is clear: People who ride bicycles spend money. While studies around the world consistently find that customers who arrive at grocery stores, convenience stores, bars, and restaurants by bicycle tend to spend more overall than people who arrive by car, the catch is that they spend less or the same amount each time they visit. They just visit more often.

As the case of Magnolia Street shows, specific improvements to streets that make them more bicycle friendly do wonders for neighborhood businesses—and business owners are taking note. After Portland's bike corrals were installed, business owners on those blocks estimated that a quarter of their customers arrived by bicycle. Five years after bike lanes went in on Valencia Street in San Francisco, two thirds of business owners on that street said that more of their customers were cyclists, that business had improved overall,[168] and they would support more traffic-calming measures.

Part of this effect is the simple fact that bikes and bike lanes have a calming effect on car traffic. When traffic on city streets is slowed down a little—even if there are the same number of cars, streets become nicer places to be. More people come there and everyone, walking, biking, or driving, has a little more freedom to look up and see what storefronts have to offer instead of focusing on staying alive. Neighborhood pride increases, as does private investment, retail sales, property values, and density of businesses. There are fewer traffic crashes. These are all quantifiable ways of saying that areas and the people in them thrive. Residents prosper, and people from other places want to visit.[169]

Yet when bike lanes, bike parking, and road diets are proposed, there is often vehement opposition—sometimes from the people who stand to benefit most.

Business owners and business-minded civic leaders are too often the last to believe that there is any value in accommodating cyclists. Even in Portland, the leaders of the city's largest business alliance recommend against any further investments in bicycle infrastructure.

Perhaps it goes back to stereotypes of cyclists as freeloaders and scofflaws. Whatever the reason, business owners do not always find it intuitive that paying customers might arrive by bicycle. Even in areas with unusually high bicycle traffic, local businesses can be the strongest resistors against any new infrastructure.

On Polk Street in San Francisco, for instance, a plan to put in a bike lane was hard fought by local merchants, since it would reduce the number of on-street parking spaces. Their plea to "Save Polk Street" was successful, and the city opted instead to paint sharrows on the street and make some improvements to intersections instead, despite the fact that only 15% of visitors to the street arrive by car.[170]

These naysayers are hardly alone. According to legend, the owner of a fancy restaurant in Manhattan objected strenuously to plans to replace some of the street parking on his block with a separated cycle track. 90% of his customers arrived by car, he claimed, and the new street configuration would put him out of business. Upon hearing this, transportation commissioner

Janette Sadik-Khan sent a staffer to stand outside that restaurant that night and ask every customer who walked through the door how they had arrived. Only 10% had driven.

In 2007, when New York City added protected bike lanes to two previously car-centric one-way arterials in Manhattan, 8th and 9th Avenues, it was a controversial move. Supporters agreed that cycling on those streets needed to be made safer if bicycles were to become a serious form of transportation in Manhattan, and that this was the best way to do it. Opponents predicted that the new infrastructure would hurt business and freight, cause crashes, hold up traffic, and waste New Yorkers' time and money. In the months after the lanes went in, several business owners complained to the press that they were losing money.

Sales tax reporting tells a different story. Sales income at locally-based businesses along 9th Avenue went up as much as 50% between 2006 and 2010. This was during a recession—in the same period, borough-wide retail sales only increased 3%. Was this entire business boom a result of the new bike infrastructure? It's impossible to say—but it is safe to suggest that the bike lane did not hurt business.

This also means that New York City business owners with storefronts that did not have good bicycle access potentially lost out on 33% of the revenues they could have earned during those four years. What small business owner wants to take that chance?

Some places are trying to stay a step ahead. Long Beach, California made national news a few years back for optimistically declaring itself to be the most bicycle friendly city in America. But they have been working hard to back up future rights to that claim; the city has been putting in bike infrastructure, including a protected bike lane on a major retail street near its eponymous beach.[171] As it builds out its infrastructure, the city has also been reaching out to business owners through its groundbreaking Bike Friendly Business District program.

The key is that they reach out before the infrastructure goes in. And they don't just ask for feedback—they get business owners involved from the beginning. The program partners with neighborhood groups to research how customers travel to a particular business district and share that information with business owners, reducing common misconceptions about who shops and how they arrive. They put on neighborhood events that encourage people to arrive by bicycle and on foot. They reimburse bike shops to offer free bicycle tune-up days—one shop declined the repayment because the day had brought in so many new, regular customers. Some businesses offer a 10% discount one day a week to customers who bicycle.

Long Beach also works with businesses that want to install good bike parking and figure out other ways to market to and encourage bicycling customers. And they provide each business with two to four bicycles for staff to use for business purposes, and each district with a cargo bike that businesses can borrow to use for deliveries, promotions, or just for fun.

It's a winning combination, and a smart one. Public processes that usually precede new infrastructure of any kind are often not particularly interactive. People affected by them are invited to comment, but are not often collaborated with.

There are many more examples of bike lanes, and bicycling in general, leading to the improvement of retail districts. As is so often the case, though, reporters never seem to have any trouble finding the disgruntled store owners who believe their business has been ruined, no matter what the aggregate experience. Not every one of them is always reasonable, but many of them are, and it's important to hear their grievances—and better to work with them ahead of time rather than after the fact.

•   •   •

As we drove into Memphis during the 2012 Dinner & Bikes tour, I felt terrible. When we arrived, it was hot and muggy out and our organizer had a surprise for us—a pedicab tour. We checked out the new bike lanes in a downtown historical district and then headed to the giant, bucolic Overton Park, where we soared down a silent, tree-lined street in the heart of the city where a freeway project had been stopped short by activists in the seventies.

I was enthralled—I had spent some time in Memphis fifteen years previously and this seemed like a different city entirely, full of greenery and people who let you cross the street without trying to run you over. But the hot sun wasn't doing me any favors, nor was the way our cheerful pedicab driver sped right over curbs and potholes. It was a relief when the tour ended and he dropped us off at a bike shop.

The shop was on the historic Broad Avenue, which had fallen on tough times until its recent revitalization as an arts district. Part of the street's rejuvenation included a new protected bike lane. Local business owners and bike advocates had worked together to paint the lane themselves, moving the block's angle-in parking spots back four feet from the curb and using a stencil to mark the lane.

There's a storied history in the U.S. of DIY bicycle infrastructure, as well as pedestrian crosswalks. Every one gets a different response. A faded hand-painted bike lane I saw in Sacramento was greeted with indifference. At the other end of the spectrum, there have been multiple cases where amateur traffic engineers caught with paint on their hands have been arrested and prosecuted.

Once in a while, though, these efforts are rewarded, and that was the case in Memphis. The "temporary redesign" of Broad Avenue was billed at first as an art project, in conjunction with a street fair that attracted 15,000 people to the street's typically sparse monthly art walk on the summer day it was unveiled. It might have just faded away over time, but the city had recently won grant funding for expanding its bike infrastructure, and it seized the opportunity to announce that it would repaint this new lane as a permanent feature.

This announcement started to transform the block in more ways, quickly attracting $6 million in development.[172] The new infrastructure would not just be on that block—the lane was expanded to connect with Overton Park and with the Shelby Farms Greenline, the city's signature off-street path, a five mile long segment of a planned bicycle superhighway that led all the way to the farm where our event that night would be. That was our next stop, by bike.

This is where my day started to really go downhill. I was light-headed and sweating buckets by the time we got as far as the Greenline. It was beautiful and there were sights to be seen—an abandoned gas station converted into a farmers market that served a low-income neighborhood, walled neighborhoods full of fancy houses surrounded by concertina wire. Our host was talking a mile a minute about the history, the dynamics, the politics of it all. I longed to hear, but he was also riding about twice as fast as I was able to on my leaden legs. He zoomed ahead, waited for me to catch up, and then took off again before I could catch my breath. The trail was full of bicycle traffic, and the gorgeous natural surroundings were set off by huge, intricate murals and sculptures. Focused on staying upright, I barely took it in.

When we arrived I downed a quart of water and somehow stayed on my feet for the rest of the night. The next morning, I felt a little better. We got in the car to drive to a breakfast place that had been recommended and I found myself back in the Memphis I remembered from long ago, the noisy, grey city with massive arterials punctuated by parking lots and all of it filled-to-bursting with hot, angry cars.

We didn't even get as far as the restaurant. We passed a gas station, and I knew we had to stop. I crawled out of the car and heaved up the meager contents of my stomach in the median. My partner hovered, concerned. Out of the corner of my eye, I saw a guy had walked up to us. "Hey, can you spare a dollar or two?" he asked. "It's not a good time, buddy," my partner said. The guy walked away, but when I finally rinsed my mouth and wedged myself back into the car, he came right back over. "How about a dollar now?"

Most narratives about the economic benefits of bicycling focus on the success stories of places like Magnolia Street in Fort Worth or Broad Avenue in Memphis. City planners, bike-friendly politicians, and bicycle advocates love to make the points that creating good bicycle access is a cost-effective way to improve certain types of retail earnings, attract creative young professionals, and raise property values in an urban business district.

Plenty of business owners are realizing the very real benefits to integrating bicycling into their business, from encouraging employees to ride to welcoming bicycling clients to advocating for safe bike routes to their door.

It's tempting for cities to focus on the low hanging fruit, improving a few streetscapes while neglecting the urgent transporation needs of people living in outlying areas. Bicycles can be a tool for building wealth and well-being, but when used as part of a flawed development plan, they can also be used to divide and segregate cities.

In Portland, the green dividend calculated by Cortright is an average. In the central city, where residents can reasonably and easily forgo car ownership entirely, it is much greater. But the outer parts of the city are a different story. These are the parts of town where poverty is concentrated and grocery stores and other daily destinations are separated by long distances and roaring roads and freeways. Bus routes out here have lately been scaled back, and bike routes are scarce. To live in these neighborhoods without a car is not a boon but a costly hardship. As Portland became world famous for bicycling, its eastern third has been left behind.

The positive results of bicycle infrastructure in a retail area are real and substantial, but they are not experienced universally. Business owners, too, are subject to forces beyond their control—the layout of streets and location of suppliers, the infrastructure available for the delivery of goods, and the transportation choices and opportunities of their employees as well as their customers.

A florist or bar may flourish when a bike lane goes in, but an auto body shop or furniture store will have a lot more adjusting to do, and we are not all—by temperament or circumstance—equally suited to accept and adapt to such changes. Any business that can be flexible has better chances to thrive—there is, for instance, a mattress shop in Portland that does booming sales by offering free bicycle delivery. But we have had many decades to grow to rely on our current diffuse, asphalt-covered ecosystem. Not everyone is going to be able to shift gears overnight.

One summer, I opened my local newspaper every day to a full-page advertisement for a well-known national big box store featuring a photo of a smiling, middle-aged woman riding a bike. The ad was clearly not intended to promote the sale of bicycles but rather to associate the company with the idea of a healthy, active, green lifestyle.

This company's stores are famously located in the most un-bike friendly areas, surrounded by vast parking lots, reliant on giant fleets of trucks to ship all of its products—including its organic ones—from thousands of miles away. The company is known for selling low-end bicycles, but not so much for lobbying for bicycle-friendly land use or road policies.

As bicycling catches on, bikes are being embraced by big business. Bicycle imagery permeates every nook of media culture. The bicycle threatens to supplant even mustaches and bacon as a badge of hipness. What use of the symbol may lack in sincerity it more than makes up for in profitability.

Whether or not this type of greenwashing—or you might call it bikewashing—contributes anything meaningful to the growing popularity of bicycle transportation is up for debate.

Big box stores, built and clustered together in massive parking lots for easy access from the freeway, are the direct descendent of the downtown department store, and are inspired by, but on a far greater scale than, the variety of mini-malls near where I grew up.

However much they might advertise bicycling and sell bicycles, they are absolutely reliant on a car-oriented landscape in order to function; and their existence serves as an anchor for continuous sprawl development. The tactics of the most successful are brutal: They price goods below cost, absorbing the losses as their competitors go out of business. Once a store becomes the only option for increasingly impoverished suburban residents to get basics like groceries and clothes, its prices go back up to market rate.

At least one of these stores has begun providing a shuttle service— essentially a privately-run transit system—so that its customers who can't afford to drive any longer can continue to do their shopping.

We all pay for this, of course, quite literally.

Our road system is in effect a subsidy for these large businesses on the outskirts of town. They occupy cheap land with lots of room for parking, easily-accessible by trucks, consolidating their operations to pay as few workers as possible as little as possible to sell us disposable goods trucked in from far away. This is an economy invented to function in sprawling exurban areas.

But these so-called discount stores are only cheaper so long as fuel remains cheap and driving and parking remain free—meaning that we pay the difference in our taxes. All while the stores soak up quite a bit of local spending, but return very little money to the economies where they are located. If we were aware of what we are paying in the true cost of what these stores sell, we would find it all a very unappealing bargain indeed.

Just as an increase in bicycle traffic compresses distances, creating density and retail clusters that strengthen communities, businesses that rely on sprawl lengthen distance and make communities diffuse and isolated. People often cite the ability to access big box stores and their savings as a primary reason that they must own a car. The math on that can't work out— can even the largest family truly save hundreds of dollars a month on the discount for buying peanut butter and diapers in bulk?

But there's more to it. Driving a car to a large department store is a recipe for buying more than we need to. Big box stores are designed to seem cheap, but to entice us into impulse purchases. When you are on a bicycle, you are less likely to go to these stores in the first place, much less decide on the spot that you need to buy new bath towels while they are on sale. You are far more likely to shop close to home. Perhaps you'll spend a little more on the same towels, but you have not purchased any gasoline along with them. Actually, you are probably more likely to wait another eight months and then spend quite a bit more on better quality towels that will last longer—and are thus cheaper in the end—than the sale ones you "missed" out on.

When bicycling, you're simply less likely to make unplanned purchases, especially large ones. Shopping, especially for bulky items, must be more carefully planned and premeditated—you'll want to do it all at once, and either bringing your trailer or renting or borrowing a car for an afternoon. Culturally, we have come to equate this with inconvenience. But more careful spending habits can create more breathing room in your wallet and your life, keep your money circulating within your community, and benefit everyone... well, everyone but the discount store shareholders. In this manner, when you ride a bicycle, you enjoy the hidden savings of spending more for things—it is so hard to see because it rests on all the things we are not buying.

That these businesses are marketing themselves using bicycle imagery is fascinating. I suspect that when push comes to shove their owners are not among the supporters of spending transportation dollars on bike lanes. And in their case, all the convincing figures in the world will only prove to them further that in a world made friendly for bicycles, they will not be able to compete.

Putting Bikes to Work

10

A 2013 report by Portland's City Club stated that expanding our bicycle infrastructure program would provide great benefits to the city—and that we should pay for it by taxing bicycle sales. Some prominent bicycle advocates have been supportive of the idea. If bicyclists prove that we can pay our way, I recently heard a city planner say, then critics won't grumble as much.

But experience shows the opposite to be true. Adding on taxes, fees, fines, and regulations is a proven strategy for making sure fewer people take up bicycling. If you want more people to ride bikes, the most effective way to go about it is not to make them pay, but to pay them to do it.

Oregon Health & Sciences University is a prominent medical school and public hospital and one of Portland's largest employers. Sitting atop a steep hill, hemmed in by narrow roads and expensive real estate, and managed with a close eye on the bottom line, OHSU is acutely attuned to the economic benefits of a cycling workforce.

In 2008, the hospital administration began handing out a $50 cash incentive for every 30 days of bike commuting an employee logs.[173] Employees can simply bike or ride in combination with transit, hopping on a bus to get across a less bike-friendly part of their commute, or using an aerial tram to get up the last steep stretch of road. Any trip of two miles or more counts.

In 2010, the first year that employees could track their trips online, more than 15% of the 120,000 person staff was enrolled in the program. Over a million miles were logged and $170,000 was paid out in incentives. Program staff estimated that since 2008, the hospital had paid employees over half a million dollars to bike to work.

Employees who participate in the program cite their physical and mental health as the top reason for cycling, closely followed by money. The main barrier to bicycling more, they say, is the dangerous roads leading to the hospital.

For the administration, the bike program, which also includes incentives like free valet bike parking, spare inner tubes, and free use of tools, is a cost-cutting measure, increasing performance and reducing days off by creating a happier and healthier staff—and is a competitive investment in comparison to building another parking garage.

Employers, small and large, have been increasingly catching on to the bottom-line benefits of bike commuting. This is no airy sustainability initiative developed to look good in marketing materials. It's about making money, pure and simple—or more to the point, it's about controlling costs.

Health may be the largest benefit, though its effects are so wide-ranging that it is difficult to analyze. Employees who have an active commute arrive at work awake, ready to go. They have a clearer head and are more productive. A study of Britain's bike economy found that workers who commute regularly by bike miss, on average, one day less of work per year.[174] Statistically, employees who qualify as obese tend to miss work for health reasons twelve times more often than those who are not and cost employers 42% more in medical care.

QBP, a bicycle parts company based in Bloomington, Minnesota, has gone the farthest to demonstrate this point. [175] The company provides employees with secure bike parking and showers, and pays workers $3 cash for every day they ride a bicycle. A quarter of employees participate, and are paid out a total of $45,000 per year. The net gain is in the company's health benefit savings. Employer health insurance premiums are rising nationwide, but QBP's dropped nearly 5% in two years, saving the company $200,000 a year. The company's insurance provider did additional analysis and estimated that the savings improved productivity and reduced sick leave resulting from the program were worth even more, at $300,000 a year. This is not a surprising figure. Researchers have determined that for every dollar a company invests into employee wellness programs like OHSU's or QBP's, it gains at least $3, and possibly twice that amount, in savings. This sort of logic may not go far in political decision making, but smart business owners are starting to take it seriously.

Employees who bike to work may, counterintuitively, have faster commutes and be more likely to arrive on time. In congested urban centers, cyclists frequently clock shorter travel times than people driving, with bike lanes and shortcuts through parks amounting to the equivalent of a carpool lane on the freeway. Being able to bypass congested traffic also means that traffic is unlikely to make you late.[176]

Perhaps the most concretely quantifiable benefit to a bike commuting workforce is parking. Providing car parking is no less formidable a cost to employers than it is to the public. Larger employers often find they must provide the most expensive type of parking—multilevel garages—to accommodate all their employees who drive to work. The enormity of this cost is lost on no one and many employers charge their employees a monthly fee for car parking—OHSU's is $150.

Yet the federal government offers a tax credit to workers who pay such fees—literally paying people to drive to work. Tax credits are available for transit pass holders as well, but no comparable incentive is offered for bicycling.[177]

Though the best workplace bicycling initiatives have a clear incentive and a mechanism to track your progress, there are other effective measures that are less cash-intensive. Indoor, secure bike parking with lockers, showers, and changing rooms are the traditional hallmark of a bike-friendly workplace. Showers are harder to manage than parking, but can be essential if employees must look professional after commuting long distances in extreme weather. Some companies go a step further, responding to employee demand by providing dry cleaning pickup and dropoff services so that cycling employees can skip the once-a-week car commute to restock their supply of fresh suits.

Other incentives range from small things like providing bike maps and having an air pump and tools available at work to keeping a company bike on hand for errands during the workday. And then there are bigger-picture factors like being in a location that is accessible by bike-friendly routes, or advocating for those routes if they do not exist. Companies without the space and money to invest in bike parking often find it makes more sense to let staff bring their bikes into the office or a storage area.

The best strategies seem to be ones that are demanded and even created by bicycling employees themselves, which is one reason workplace-based bike commute challenges seems to be so universally effective at normalizing bicycling and producing new bike commuters. Whether run by advocacy groups or internally, these friendly competitions provide incentives for people to learn from each other about how to make use of whatever bicycling infrastructure and resources are available.

• • •

Sitting in a Portland, Oregon restaurant one morning in 2009, I glanced out the window and saw a shipment of produce being unloaded—from a giant box on the back of a tricycle.

I did a double take. What I was witnessing was one of the original box trikes of B-Line, the city's newest freight delivery company.

Nowadays, you see these vehicles all over town, pulled up to unload a week's worth of produce at a local restaurant or a shipment of fresh baguettes or energy drinks to the food co-op. Impossibly cheerful pedalers power up to 600 pounds of cargo around town, aided on the uphills by an electric assist—which, unlike a motorcycle engine, is designed to supplement pedaling and can't go faster than an unassisted rider on a lighter bike.

One of their first clients was a produce distributor based in Eugene. A truck would bring the day's fresh vegetables up to B-Line's warehouse in Portland, and the box trikes would take it from there, navigating city streets to make a dozen deliveries a day. Then they signed with a large, local coffee roastery. Then a national beverage company. Their banner moment came when they won a competitive contract to deliver all of the city's and a local university's office supplies. The economy has gone nowhere but down the tubes since they opened, yet their company has grown from two employees to thirteen.

B-Line's box trikes have a lot of advantages over larger trucks. They don't need to park on the street, but can nimbly be unloaded directly at the door of their destination. Taking smaller loads on shorter runs allows them to operate faster and with competitive, though not necessarily cheaper, pricing.

By 2013, B-Line had six trikes, making over 150 deliveries a day for over a dozen clients, is on track to do $400,000 in annual revenue,[178] and is courting investors to help bring the business model to other cities.

Obviously this isn't a freight solution for every need, but the market has spoken: Bicycle freight fills a real niche, and fills it better than the competition. And they contribute something to the city that regular trucking companies can't: B-Line's vehicles emit no plumes of smoke and no noise louder than a subtle whir, the ring of a bell, and a friendly hello.

B-Line isn't the only bicycle delivery company in Portland. Businesses large and small are testing the waters, and several are blossoming.

But bikes won't ever replace freight, right? It's amazing how often that comes up, like the punchline of a bad joke, meant to prove for once and for all that bicycling isn't a viable form of anything. "How do you think your food gets delivered?" is a standard response to any discussion, no matter how modest in nature, about the benefits of bicycling.

The clear answer is that in a more bike friendly climate, food—and other imported goods—would probably still be delivered in a truck—it would just get there faster and be stuck in far less traffic on the way there. A glut of single-occupancy vehicles is the shared frustration of truck drivers and cyclists.[179]

In practice, the relationship is not always so congenial. Trucks with tractor trailers pose a grave danger on shared roads—not just to people bicycling, but to people driving, walking, and waiting for the bus. In some cities, this basic incompatibility of heavy freight with urban life is recognized. In Japan, for instance, depots for large trucks are on the outskirts of cities, and loads are delivered to their final destination in smaller box trucks.

In London, trucks are involved in nearly half of cycling fatalities. The mayor, Boris Johnson, after he was nearly killed by a truck in an incident that was caught on tape and made worldwide news, proposed in 2010 to ban all large trucks from central London. Heavy trucks would unload outside the city, as in Japan, and goods would be delivered in more appropriate sized vehicles. He only partly succeeded—large trucks are now banned on city streets at night. But the issue has come up again three years later after a top climate scientist was killed by a left-turning heavy truck, and the law may go through this time. Johnson didn't mention cargo bikes in his plans for London's freight future, but companies like B-Line are perfectly suited for a role in this new ecosystem.

Bicycles and their three-wheeled cousins are already a major piece of the freight puzzle all over the world—from rural coffee plantations in Central America to the streets of any city where small and micro businesses thrive. In U.S. cities, we have much to learn from the Global South, not least in this arena. Still, bicycle freight has never quite fallen completely by the wayside in America. We have a long history of bicycle delivery of pizza and sandwiches. A handful of small companies use bicycles to collect recycling and compostables. Bicycle messengers are a normal fixture of city life, carrying items large and small—things that simply can't be emailed and that have to get there fast. Most messenger companies employ drivers for long hauls, but inner-city deliveries can't be made expediently when traffic and parking must be navigated in a car.

Other businesses are starting to use bicycles for work that a truck would have done previously. A few years ago, I was walking past the campus of a small university near my home and spotted a cargo tricycle filled with landscaping equipment. A university staffer told me that they had replaced their small fleet of pickup trucks with these bicycles, which did the job just as well and provided a safer and quieter environment for students.

Most bike-based businesses are by nature small or medium-sized. With their low overhead and replacement of fuel with human power, they provide something that is sorely needed right now—jobs. Bike delivery can't be automated or outsourced—you need a human being, hauling a human-scaled load all over town to make these operations work.

When places thrive, people and goods simply don't have to travel as far. Laura Crawford and Russ Roca, on the other hand, choose to go on long bicycle trips and can bring their work with them. They went on their first bike tour in 2009, pedaling through the desert in Joshua Tree National Park with camping gear, food, and water strapped to their racks. "What if we just kept riding?" they asked each other. Later that year they made what seemed like a rash decision. They left their apartment in Santa Monica, California and sold their belongings, and set off to ride their bikes around the country without plans for where they would end up or when they would return. They brought the tools of their trade to support themselves along the way—Roca is a photographer and Crawford is a fine metalworker.[180]

Everywhere they went, they organized events at bike shops and bars to share the story of their trip and give advice and encouragement to other would-be bicycle travelers. The events were well-attended. Crawford and Roca's message was perfectly timed to have broad appeal. Bicycle travel is at once about affordable family vacations and rural economic development, two things that are hard to come by in a down economy. It brings other things that people crave as well: the satisfaction of self-reliance, heartwarming encounters with strangers, and the sheer fun of rolling down empty roads through beautiful countryside.

Four years later, they are still touring for much of the year, though they live in an apartment again. They've found a new line of work, as well, that draws on the experience and knowledge they gained on the road—working with tourism agencies to tell the world about the joys of bike travel, and helping small towns market themselves and provide bicycle-specific hospitality.

Their main message is bold but simple: bicycle tourism can help save rural America.

As anyone who has been to Disneyworld knows, a dense, walkable Main Street is something that a lot of people will pay good money to visit, especially if there are roller coaster rides involved. I submit that bicycling fulfills both these desires: community and pleasure.

It's not just tourists; when you look at the choices of people who have the freedom to live anywhere they want, whether because their job is location independent or because they are independently wealthy or retired, you see a strong trend towards bustling but not-too-dense urban neighborhoods of the sort that also happen to be bicycle friendly.

Bicycle tourism itself is a big money maker for similar reasons. Whole economies spring up around bicycle-laden beach boardwalks and trailheads. Businesses are launched to house, feed, transport, and delight people who come to spend a weekend sleeping late and going on leisurely bike rides in nature. These businesses, just like urban retail next to a bike lane, tend to be locally owned and to direct a large part of their revenues back into local communities that often lack other industries.

Recreational cycling alone contributes $81 billion to the national economy every year. In the Outer Banks of North Carolina, $60 million a year is generated from tourists who come to the area just to ride bikes—nine times the initial cost of building the area's bicycle infrastructure. Even accounting for maintenance and expansion, that's a great multiplier.[181] Recreational bicycling and bicycle tourism in Wisconsin and Colorado are estimated to bring each state one billion dollars every year.

A study in Oregon estimated that of the state's $9 billion tourism economy, $400 million came from recreational bicycle travel—mostly people going on daylong rides on back country roads or participating in organized rides and events. Attempts to encourage more of such travel have been fruitful. One of Oregon's most popular destinations, Crater Lake National Park, is beloved by visitors on bikes and in cars, but the experience of sharing the narrow road around the lake's perimeter can be frustrating and distracting for both. The state experimented in June 2013 with making half the perimeter route carfree for a day. On less than a week's notice, cyclists flooded to the area from all over the state. Park employees said it was the best day of the season to date. That translated well into the local economy, with the cyclists staying in hotels and buying picnic provisions and restaurant meals at local businesses. The carfree day will now be an annual event.

In Oregon, one event alone is responsible for about $5 million of that bicycle tourism income, and it gives much of that money back in an unusually direct way. Cycle Oregon is a week-long organized ride with thousands of participants. Their fees go into a fund that helps pay for projects, from bike lanes to parking to guide books, that improve cycling conditions and attract cycle tourists to rural parts of the state. The rides, which follow a different route every year, are a bonanza for the rural towns they pass through, with restaurants, stores, and hotels doing brisk business shoulder-to-shoulder with farms selling their produce, churches putting on massive spaghetti dinners, and families selling chocolate milk and ice cream by the roadside. Many of these towns report benefits that persist after each ride, as participants who catch the bike-touring bug are eager to return.

Iowa also has a thriving bicycle economy, in no small way due to their own massive, multi-day annual event: RAGBRAI, or the Register's Annual Great Big Ride Across Iowa. A roving party with 10,000 participants, the ride has become so popular since its 1973 inception that entry is awarded by lottery. As in Oregon, the event has put bicycle touring on the radar for Iowans and produced bicycle-friendly destinations around the state. As a result, the annual economic impacts of recreational cycling in the state of Iowa clock in at $365 million—it's as if Iowans were paid a million dollars a day just to have fun on bikes.[182] Specific investments are paying off as well—in the last two years, the state has spent less than $3 million a year on recreational bike trails, and seen a $21 million a year increase in sales tax revenue along those trails as a result.

Free-form, self-supported bicycle touring is becoming more popular throughout the country. Instead of waiting or paying to participate in big rides that cart your gear for you in a van, an increasing number of people are spending their vacations riding their local back roads, staying in small-town motels or packing camping gear in their bike panniers. This is the type of travel of which Crawford and Roca have become the unofficial ambassadors.

Bike touring has a different kind of economic impact than the modern day road trip. Traveling long distances in a car, you're more likely to make quick stops at freeway exits en route to your destination. Most of the money you spend on fuel and at chain stores immediately leaves the local economy. While bike touring, you go slower, see more, and stop more often. You don't always spend as much money, especially if you're on a budget and camping. But your small purchases—an apple here, an ice cream cone there, an entire pizza and a giant salad and two beers at the end of the day—put your cash straight into local circulation in rural towns that have been in deep decline for decades.

One researcher found that there are two kinds of bicycle tourists, occupying two ends of a spectrum.[183] There are those who spend very little, camping and cooking their own food. As a group, their economic contribution is not insubstantial, going to local grocery stores, roadside stands, campgrounds, and hostels. The second type of bicycle tourist has more disposable income. They are likely to partake of luxuries like wine tastings, restaurant meals, stops at museums and other attractions, and comfortable stays in bed and breakfasts. Though they are willing to spend big, they often still find bicycle touring to be more economical than if they were paying for gas and staying in urban hotels. Both types of bike tourist are more likely to support local businesses—particularly since these are the businesses they are most likely to discover along their rural routes.

As interest in bicycle tourism grows, how do communities better capture this money? Businesses can go out of their way to welcome day riders or cycle tourists in a number of small ways. Seasoned bicycle tourists say it's fairly simple. They appreciate good, secure bike parking out of the elements, being greeted by a smile rather than a frown when they walk into a store drenched from a rain storm and perhaps covered in bike grease from a mechanical issue, and businesses that have maps on hand and a ready knowledge of bike-friendly directions around town.

Clearly a lot of people like to ride bicycles—it is the third most popular recreational activity in the U.S. after fishing and running.[184] Encouraging this inclination isn't rocket science. The conditions that make recreational trails so enticing and the ones that make people eager to pay to participate in organized events are similar to the conditions that lead to more transportation riding.

Easy access to a clearly-marked route that is relatively free of car traffic brings people out to ride country roads in droves. And there is also the factor of community and official support: things like maps, encouragement, and the knowledge that if you break down or something unexpected happens someone will come to your aid or you'll be able to get where you're going by other means.

Bicycle tourism provides a strong example of the latent demand for good bicycling conditions, and the prosperity that comes with them. Many rural areas are leading the way when it comes to bicycling. Their urban and suburban neighbors would do well to take notice.

Whose Streets, Indeed?

Jenna Burton moved to Oakland, California in 2007. She was tired of the cost and hassle of driving and the thriving bicycle culture in the Bay Area inspired her to get on a bicycle for the first time since she was nine. She loved it, and took to it in part because in Oakland, and especially in her activist circle, it was a normal way to get around.[185]

But her friends from back home thought it was a strange choice to make. And she noticed one thing right away—there weren't that many other people on bikes who looked like her. Even though 28% of the city's population is African American, the few other Black people she did see on bikes were mostly using them as a last resort, a far cry from her own exuberant choice.

It was up to her, she decided, to create a space for more Black folks to try out bikes and develop a bicycling culture. She invited her friends to join her on a weekend ride. The response was enthusiastic, but only two others showed up. They had a great time on the ride and she decided to continue and try to build momentum.

In 2010, Burton and a core group of organizers officially launched Red, Bike, and Green. "It's bigger than bikes" is one of the group's slogans. The three points of their mission make this clear: They promote and use bicycles as a tool to help Black people be healthier and more active, to save money and support Black-owned businesses, and work to reduce pollution and other environmental factors that disproportionately affect Black folks.

R.B.G. began in earnest with a monthly ride that coincided with the city's First Friday arts walk. In diverse Oakland, the art event was predominantly white, and Burton's group of dozens of young riders took delight in riding through it with their Black Critical Mass. The group soon established a second monthly ride, held on a weekend and paced for families. Over the winter, they held indoor events to socialize with each other and prospective new cyclists. A main focus from the start was on creating art around R.B.G., developing a strong visual identity for the growing community.

As the word spread, and as members moved to other cities, other Black cycling organizations got in touch to collaborate. Active chapters of R.B.G. sprang up in Atlanta, Chicago, and New York, each with its own character and focus. Several of the chapters are expanding their outreach activities, giving away bicycles, teaching bike repair, and doing events focused around art and music. They all take care to support Black-owned businesses, despite—and because of—not being located in the most bike-friendly parts of town.

Eboni Senai Hawkins founded the Chicago branch of R.B.G. after moving there from Oakland. While the Oakland group is intent on building a cohesive Black cycling identity in a diverse city, Senai Hawkins' focus is on creating connections—the group holds joint rides with other Black cycling clubs and a Puerto Rican riding group, tours urban gardens in African American neighborhoods, and tries to reach out and promote the benefits of cycling to other Black people who aren't always invited or included by the cycling mainstream. "Cycling for us is a community-building tool," she told local radio station WBUR. "So when people see—they actually see—black people on bikes, who look like them, that goes a long way."[186]

The Atlanta group has taken yet a different tack, focusing on more traditional advocacy. They had a major success in 2012, when a planned bicycle corridor would have skipped over Sweet Auburn, the city's oldest African American neighborhood.[187] R.B.G. mobilized the community, organizing a bike tour of the neighborhood and circulating a letter from local residents and business owners. The campaign worked, and the city pledged to include Auburn Avenue in the bike network.

Until recently, there has been a myth, both tacit and stated, among bicycle advocates, that people of color don't want to bike. A growing number of groups like R.B.G. are proving otherwise. So is recent census data.

People of color make up the fastest-growing demographic among cyclists, reports the League of American Bicyclists.[188] Bicycle commute rates among African Americans are growing the fastest, doubling in the last decade—by contrast, there has been only a 22% increase in bike commuters who identify as white. Hispanic and Asian commuting rates are also growing fast, at 50% and 80% respectively.

The same trend is reflected in the bicycle industry research. Spending at bike shops by white customers, at whom the bike industry overwhelmingly directs its marketing prowess, increased all of 6% between 2000 and 2010. In the same period, African American customers spent 12% more than before, and Asian and Latino customers increased their spending on bikes and gear by 43%.

Immigrants, wherever they are from, are twice as likely as people born in the U.S. to ride a bike. Immigrants with low incomes who live in dense residential neighborhoods are ten times more likely to. Many people who move to the U.S. come from places where bicycling is the norm, though everyone who moves here tends to transition away from bicycling after living here for a few years.[189]

Some advocates have been surprised by these findings, but not all. "This is the new normal," bicycling anthropologist Adonia Lugo told me. We were discussing Red, Bike, and Green and other groups that are, as Lugo puts it, taking bicycles and incorporating them into their own lives, building their own cultures around them.

The idea of normalizing bicycling has great cachet among advocates. For instance, a cycling blogger based in Copenhagen insists that people ought to only wear "normal" clothes to ride bikes, such as suits for men, high heels and skirts for women, and helmets for neither. But, Lugo points out, while this attire is normal both on and off the bicycle in Denmark, when the idea is exported it takes on new meanings. A lot of women in the U.S., for instance, rarely dress up and never wear high heels for any purpose, much less to bike; so this vision of normalcy often falls flat as a way to sell bicycling. In the U.S., we have long assumed that normal cyclists look a certain way—white, male, wearing sport clothes.

This focus on normalcy and mainstreaming has led many U.S. bicycle advocates to become positively allergic to anything that smacks of bicycle culture or community. Some have gone so far as to argue that forming subcultures around bicycling is elitist and exclusive, and that their existence is what is preventing bicycling from increasing even more quickly.

But people like to form communities around their passionate interests and their idea of fun, whether that is bikes, cars, or something else entirely. In bicycling, these groups are often seeking anything but normalcy and blending into mainstream culture. For everyone who just wants to ride their bike to the grocery store and be left alone, there seem to be others for whom the bicycle is a way to visibly and effectively buck the status quo, whether that is represented by cars, unhealthy lifestyles, racial or gender identities, the oil economy, or the social demands of work and parenthood. Even better, bicycling can be a way to meet others who share your beliefs about these topics. Many of these groups are exclusive in that they are limited to members who share a specific identity or interest. But by calling into question what is normal and making alternatives visible, they are greatly expanding the possibilities of who can be included and who can be a leader.

The Ovarian Psycos are a powerful example of a group that has made bicycling very much their own, while opening up huge new possibilities for what it can mean to be a bicyclist.[190] The Ovas are mostly Chicana women in their early twenties, many of them artists and community organizers, who began in 2010 as a safe space "for young women of color who refuse to accept the status quo." To the Ovas, organizing bicycle rides and events is a natural means toward "healing our communities physically, emotionally, and spiritually." They got off to a bumpy start—on their very first ride, their founder hit a pothole and crashed, hitting her face on the pavement and spending a week in the hospital. Horrified, half of the riders never came back. The other half stayed; after that, nothing would faze them.

"Ovaries so big we don't need no fucking balls!" is their rallying cry. Their short monthly Luna Rides are slow, friendly, and built to make beginners feel welcome and comfortable. Each ride has a theme and a destination, be it a self-defense workshop or a discussion about domestic violence, gang culture, or young runaways and child abuse—topics with personal importance to many members. The Ovas provide leadership beyond their group as well. They have hosted a ride and discussion for male allies, as well as a response to Critical Mass called Clitoral Mass, which brought out over 200 women and woman-identified people to its inaugural night in 2012. They are also working to open a community bike shop in their neighborhood, Boyle Heights, which will serve as a physical anchor for the group and a way to reach out to the broader community.

Perhaps because of the myth that they don't want to bike, communities of color are often passed over when it comes to bicycle investments and outreach. Until recently the term "invisible cyclists" was used by advocates to describe cyclists of color who commute during hours that cause them not to be seen by the middle class; a staggeringly insensitive assessment of who is seen, who is overlooked, and why. Racial assumptions aside, this is in part because nobody is looking—on-street bicycle counts rarely include race or ethnicity as factors. This blind spot on the part of bicycling leaders has also, in many cases, proven to be a self-fulfilling prophecy.

There has never been anything inherently white about bicycling. But going all the way back to 1894, when the League passed its infamous color bar, very real barriers to healthy transportation choices have been systematically placed squarely in front of communities of color. [191]

The data bears this out as well. There is inequality along race and class lines in access to bicycle-friendly streets—and to bicycles themselves.[192] Bike-share programs have been criticized for rarely installing stations in low-income neighborhoods, and not promoting them to diverse communities; unsurprisingly, program membership tends to be overwhelmingly white.

Poor urban neighborhoods are less likely than wealthier areas nearby to have any bicycle lanes or other infrastructure, and less likely to enjoy the sort of bike-friendly road diet that is bringing increased prosperity to retail districts around the country. A Los Angeles study looked closer at the data and found that in neighborhoods with the highest percentage of people of color, bike lanes were fewer and farther between. Residents of lower income neighborhoods (with ethnicity often being a significant factor) are less likely to be already active and in good health than their wealthier neighbors, they have higher levels of traffic noise, dangerous streets with higher rates of crashes, and often abysmally-bad air quality. Areas with the lowest household incomes are where you find the most crashes involving people walking or riding bicycles. Black and Hispanic people have about a 25% greater risk than Caucasians of being killed while cycling.

This is changing slowly, thanks to the leadership and visibility of groups like R.B.G., the Ovarian Psycos, and countless others.

People of color, the League's report found, are riding bikes in greater numbers and are generally supportive of bicycling. They are as overwhelmingly likely as white people to have a positive view of cyclists. They also, when asked, are more likely to express concerns about traffic safety and to support greater public investment in bicycle infrastructure. Both people of color and people with lower incomes across the board say they are more likely to start riding bicycles if they have access to secure bicycle parking, a cycling club to join, and a way to learn safe riding skills.

Sure enough, when there is infrastructure, people will use it no matter what their race or class. Few studies of infrastructure effectiveness take race into account, but a New Orleans study did: It found that in 2010[193] a new bike lane painted onto New Carrollton Street, in a racially and economically-diverse urban neighborhood, increased the amount of cycling among all populations. The number of women riding on that street more than doubled, and there was a fifty percent increase of African American riders.

One thing is clear: The coming advances in the bicycle movement are going to require new leaders, a shift which is already happening. The relative monoculture of bicycle advocacy leadership over the decades has taken its toll.

It's often too easy for the privileged to assume that one's own issues and barriers are universal, and to be blind to barriers that don't apply to us. Until recently, most leading bicycle advocates, planners, and decision makers in the U.S. have backgrounds that allow them to take certain things for granted—to be able to replace a bike that is stolen, or get good service at a bike shop, or be treated fairly by a police officer, or be well represented in court when they get a ticket.

People outside the fold of established advocacy often can't expect these things as a matter of course. If asked, they might identify different issues and locations to focus advocacy efforts on. All too often, though, they are not asked.

Asking, however, can bear fruit. Several years ago, the Community Cycling Center, a nonprofit bike shop in Portland, re-examined its mission and decided to shift its focus away from the shop's rapidly-gentrifying neighborhood. Instead, they reached out to communities of color farther away, particularly residents of two large subsidized housing developments. Four women who lived at a development in Northeast Portland called Hacienda liked the idea of improving bicycling in their community. They decided to work with the CCC to create a new organization, *Andandos in Bicicletas en Cully*.

The new group's first act was to survey residents about bicycling—what they wanted and needed. It turned out that people at Hacienda wanted to bike much more than they actually did. The biggest barrier was a lack of bike parking. Bikes were prohibited inside people's apartments; they had to be stored out in the elements and there was a high rate of bike theft. Nearly every household had lost at least one bicycle to thieves and many had given up on replacing the stolen bikes with new ones, not wanting only to see those stolen in turn.

A.B.C.'s first priority was clear—raising funds to build a bike shed. While they did that, they set about training residents to fix flat tires, find good routes, and other basic bike transportation skills. The trainees then become the teachers, passing their new skills along to others in the community.

Perhaps one reason that so much of the new energy in cycling is coming from communities of color is that the barriers are higher, help is less forthcoming, and the injustice is all the more stark.

Meanwhile, the establishment is starting to open its eyes, to not just see but listen to and be led by these community bicycle movements. Their rise provides new opportunities for leadership—and proves the effectiveness of people riding together and using bicycles to change the shape of their own neighborhoods and communities.

•   •   •

In 2009, Emily Finch was in her early thirties, living in the small town of Williamsport, Pennsylvania.[194] Her husband was in his medical residency, and she was raising five children with another one on the way. She wasn't happy. She knew that something in her life had to change, but she didn't know what.

One day an Internet search turned up a picture of a *bakfiets*, a type of Dutch bicycle that literally means "box bike." The bikes are nine feet long, weigh 100 pounds unloaded, cost $3,000, and come equipped with a hardwood box in the front with a bench for children. This was the thing that would change her life, Finch decided.

When the bike arrived, she loaded up the kids to pedal the half mile to her husband's work. The bike wobbled mightily; she could barely pedal it. She thought she'd made the most expensive mistake of her life.

But she kept going, taking the lane in Williamsport's uncrowded but not-very-friendly streets. As it slowly became easier to ride, her depression lifted. Within a year she was riding everywhere confidently and sold her nine-seater SUV. Then the family moved to Portland, Oregon, purely for its bicycling reputation.

In Portland, they found their people. Her new neighborhood seemed full of other cycling families—her kids' new friends always had helmets with them, so they could arrange impromptu pickups and trips to the park. Getting stronger, Emily biked around Portland's hilly landscape, now with six kids, and, often enough, a massive load of groceries or a case of wine in tow—she estimates that her whole rig weighs as much as 550 pounds, even though her oldest can now ride separately on his own bike.

A story on the local BikePortland blog launched her into a sort of international celebrity. Her story showed people around the world that bicycling with children could be a real possibility, and fun besides.

Back In the 1890s, the bicycle was a powerful force in the liberation of women. It was the perfect vehicle for the first golden age of feminism to unfold, providing a self-sufficient escape from the constraints of domestic life, not to mention the restrictive heavy skirts and corsets of the time.

But by 1905 the more expensive motor car had become king. A century later, when I was first getting involved with bicycle activism, biking had become largely the realm of men. This was particularly true in the sports side of bicycling and in the industry that supported it.

But among those who rode bicycles for transportation there was also a clear gender gap. And as getting around by bicycle became more popular, that gap wasn't shrinking, as you might expect—it was getting wider. The new riders out there on the roads represented all races, classes, and ethnicities—but they were mostly men. Except in the most bicycle-friendly cities like Minneapolis and Portland, women seemed to be increasingly leaving the bike behind.[195]

In fact, the primary demographic barrier to getting on a bicycle, at least to go to work, appears to be gender.

Why is this? Everyone seems to have a theory. As with race, there was until recently a pervasive idea that women just don't want to bike.

As with race, women's inherent disinterest in bicycling has proven to be a myth, in large part thanks to a recent surge in advocacy and organizing around bicycling by groups of women.

It turns out that women want to ride bicycles just as much as men—but the barriers that prevent us haven't been addressed or even seen by past leaders in the bicycle movement.

The long and ignoble history of race in the U.S. persists in inequality of opportunity as well as geographic segregation. Both affect transportation choices. When you add gender to the analysis, the inequality grows greater across the board.

Women are disproportionately constrained by poverty. We still don't earn equal pay—we make, on average, 77 cents for each dollar earned by men doing equivalent work. When you break that pay gap down by race it becomes more stark. In 2010, according to the Bureau of Labor Statistics, white women earned 81 cents for every dollar earned by a white man. Black men earned 75 cents on that same dollar, Black women earned 70 cents, and Hispanic men and women earned 66 and 60 cents, respectively.

Factors in this wage gap range from outright wage discrimination to the vastly different kinds of work available to women and men of different racial identities. The U.S. is one of the few countries in the world that does not provide paid maternity leave, and there also remains a hiring bias against pregnant women and mothers. When you add it all up, women, particularly women of color, are more likely to live in poverty. With poverty comes all the economic constraints that limit both housing and transportation choices. People with lower incomes are more likely to be stuck in inaccessible suburbs or troubled urban neighborhoods, living in the midst of the noise and bad air near busy roads, with a lack of access to bicycles, decent routes to ride them on, and secure places to park them.

Then there is unpaid labor. There are a lot of different kinds of work, and there is no bike-to-work cash incentive program for the unpaid, household, and parenting labor that still largely falls on women's shoulders. Household work is not distributed equally. In 2004, a research team found that married women reported an average of one more hour of housework per day than their male partners—even when both worked full time. The same women reported spending twice the time caring for young children as did the men.[196]

The gender division of labor used to be far more stark than it is today. In 1973, with the age of the automobile in full swing, 70% of adults without access to cars were women. The labor model popularized by Henry Ford, in which a well-paid male work force was supported domestically by wives, who in turn they supported as well as all the expenses of living in single-family homes well-equipped with the electronic consumer appliances that were fueling much of the country's economic growth at the time.

At least, that was the dream. The reality was never so rosy, as was so scathingly chronicled in Betty Friedan's *The Feminine Mystique*. And even its imperfect incarnation was available only to a relatively wealthy middle class of mostly white women. This dream also proved unsustainable as a national economic model. By the 1960s, many of these suburban single-family households needed two incomes to function. Women returned to the workforce but typically still did most of the unpaid labor, in effect working double shifts; but this change came with added expenses, including day care for children—and a second car.

Nowadays, these double responsibilities add up to complicated transportation needs. Women make more trips than men, with diverse kinds of trips chained together. And twice as many trips are at the service of passengers—the school drop-off, soccer practice, and the playdate wedged in there between the grocery run and the commute to work. No wonder the minivan is inextricably linked with motherhood in America.

Most bicycles sold in the U.S. are designed for light weight and speed, and are not equipped with amenities like luggage racks and built-in lights. And these bikes are the ones that are most compatible with the speed and distances of our roads. Riding a fast road on a fast bike, navigating traffic and getting a good workout is one thing; a *bakfiets* or even a regular bike with a child seat cannot be pedaled nearly as fast. It's a very different experience to travel on even a moderately busy road at 18 miles per hour than it is at only 8.

When women do cycle, researchers find, we are somewhat more likely than men to demand and use protected bike lanes. It makes good sense. Who would not prefer to carry children, heavy cargo, or even just our regular-old cycling selves on streets free from fast car traffic? When those options aren't available, it isn't surprising that the vast majority of Americans balk at cycling, whatever our gender.

A small minority of the population will always be happy to test their mettle against fast traffic; most of us need to get where we are going in one piece, and for that we need streets we can actually ride on at a human speed, whatever we are carrying.

In places where the streets are not meant for cycling, it's not a surprise that men are more likely to choose a bike as an economical alternative to driving.[197] Measures that improve bicycling safety and comfort aren't just a women's issue, though—good streets for bikes are good for everyone. The fact that women are taking the lead in advocating for such streets is a result of social and economic inequality, not of inherent preferences, fears, or biological imperatives.

In places where bicycling is the norm, there is no gender gap at all. In northern Europe, sexism and racism are alive and well in various forms, but everyone rides bicycles at pretty much equal rates.[198] In the U.S., the gender gap is smallest in the best cycling cities.

In fact, the rates of women and people of color who ride bicycles may be higher than current data reflects. Remember, the census measures only commute trips; in the current economic climate this makes it a particularly inaccurate way to count people who are particularly economically vulnerable. A survey of women who ride bicycles in Seattle, for instance, found that three of their top five bicycle destinations included stores, errands, and social visits—trips that are difficult to count through traditional measures.[199] Generational changes are afoot as well—60% of bicycle owners age 28 and younger are women.[200]

If you want to know how to open up bicycling to the population at large, look no farther than the people who have the greatest barriers but are out there riding anyway. In nearly every case, this will show you two trends. First, people want to ride, but will not do so in great numbers without access to bicycle-specific infrastructure, be it protected bike lanes or a bike-share system. Second, group rides and cultural movements, organized at the grassroots level, are the greatest force there is in growing the bicycle movement and creating unstoppable demand for better streets.

Bicycling has the potential to be a great equalizer. It requires only minor infrastructure investments and social shifts to be a powerful tool for us to redraw the lines in our society that determine far more than how we reach our destinations.

Whatever demographic gaps persist within bicycling, they are small in comparison to a far-more-serious gap—the one between the 70% of people who want to bicycle and the one to ten percent who actually do.[201] And it is the people who are newest to the table who are, as is so often the case, bringing the boldest visions and the most effective plans.

Human Infrastructure

At 20, I was living without a car in New Haven, Connecticut, a few miles from the suburb where I grew up. Rummaging for old furniture in my parents' garage one day, I found my old purple childhood bike, rusty but still serviceable after a decade of disuse. A little air and grease from the bike shop down the street and I was rolling. When I'd been a kid, the bike was too large to handle comfortably, but now it fit me perfectly.

The bike was fun to ride, and it expanded my horizons. It cut my two mile commute from a 45 minute trek to a 15 minute joyride. I bought a wire basket for the front and could carry a bag of groceries in it. I gleefully rode everywhere, wrong-way riding, red light running, and terrorizing pedestrians—I had no idea what I was doing.

One day on the way to work I made a stop at the bank. Leaving, I rode directly off the ten-inch curb into the street, intending to cross midblock as a shortcut. Instead, my bike landed with a crash, bucking me off. I sat in the street for a few seconds. I wasn't hurt but my bike chain had fallen off. A man walking by had stopped to assess my situation as well. "Good try," he said, "but if you want to hop curbs like that, you need wider tires." Then he kept walking.

His comment stuck with me. It was the first time I had considered that it wasn't just me, roaming around the city on two wheels trying to stay out of trouble—other people rode bikes and knew about them and thought about them in a systematic way. I knew that riding was fun, but this was the moment I decided that it was also cool, not just something I did, but something I was part of.

I got to work with chain grease all over my hands and a smudged but distinctive sprocket-shaped grease mark on my left leg. It didn't wash off with soap, but I didn't mind. I was proud. I told everyone at work the story and spent the rest of the day trying to sit so that my marked leg was visible to anyone walking by.

Three years later, in 2001, I moved to Portland, Oregon. The city was not the bicycle paradise it is now, but it was already fairly normal to ride a bike. I definitely wasn't such a weirdo to think it was cool to have bike grease on me. And after I started meeting people with black chainring marks tattooed permanently on their calves, proudly wearing the badge, I knew I wasn't the only one who'd had their first glimmer of community in that sign.

In 2009, Adonia Lugo interviewed a wide range of Los Angeles bicycle advocates for her doctorate in anthropology.[202] To her surprise, she found a common thread—all their stories led back to Critical Mass.

Critical Mass was invented in San Francisco in 1992. It was envisioned as a pedal-powered city bus, a way to turn a lonely and embattled daily bike commute into a festive group ride on the last Friday of every month.

The guiding principles were simple. The rides were fun, billed as a "defiant celebration." They were leaderless and had no route; anyone with vision and charisma could choose where the ride would turn and where it would end up. There was no official message or mission. The ride grew quickly in San Francisco and beyond, delighting and confounding residents of cities all over the world.

Critical Mass is an example of what Lugo has termed "human infrastructure." Whether or not bike lanes or other physical types of bicycle infrastructure exist, it's the people using them who ultimately make streets what they are. Just as streets influence our culture, the culture we create defines how streets are used. We humans have as much or more impact on the shape and speed of our world than concrete, paint, and laws.

In Los Angeles in the 1990s, bicycling conditions were terrible. Though it enjoyed a golden age of bicycling a century ago, L.A. today is a sprawling, disconnected city. It was a challenge to connect with like-minded souls, pedaling alone down the city's congested boulevards.

The first Critical Mass in Los Angeles was in 1997, with five bold riders proudly taking back the streets. Slowly, the movement took off. Riders invited their friends and connected with other groups, mainly environmentalists. The monthly ride soon grew to 40 people, then hundreds.

It was those early rides, and some later ones, that brought together the people with the ideas, energy, and vision for bicycles. The rides created a space for new leaders to find a voice, connected existing groups, and planted the seeds that would eventually grow into the varied landscape that is today's thriving bicycle scene in Los Angeles. The founders of the area's mainstream bicycle advocacy group, the Los Angeles County Bicycle Coalition, met at Critical Mass. The city's proliferation of bicycle co-ops rose out of the network created by Critical Mass. Out of these co-ops sprang the Midnight Ridazz, a thousands-strong monthly nighttime ride that now fills the role of the city's largest grassroots bicycle celebration.

Lugo herself tapped into these networks in her own contributions to LA's bicycle advocacy ecosystem. While living in a housing co-operative with several of the original Critical Mass participants. she and a partner took the lead in organizing CicLAvia, the city's first open streets event.

Open streets events, first called *ciclovías*, originated in Bogotá, Colombia in the 1970s, and have been spreading like wildfire through North American cities for the past five years. A *ciclovía* is usually on a weekend afternoon, during which a one to ten mile loop of roads is closed to cars and opened to people walking and bicycling. The route is usually chosen to connect wealthy and poor parts of the city alike, and to include many parks, where free dance and exercise classes are taught throughout the day.

Unlike Critical Mass, open streets events are sanctioned and often organized by the city. Everyone wins, including local businesses along the way, which report huge spikes in sales. Like Critical Mass, they serve as a rare opportunity for residents to step out onto major streets and enjoy them in safety and camaraderie, often noticing the architecture along the way and the true scale of the city for the first time as they move under their own power. Both types of events capture participants' imagination in a lasting way and provide a new vision of what streets are and who they are for.

The first CicLAvia was in October, 2010. Over 100,000 people came out to walk or bike the route. The event, along with bicycling in L.A., has grown in size and popularity since.

Like Los Angeles, Seattle is becoming a great city to get around by bike. Its residents know it—in the last several years they have been taking to two wheels like fish to water, and bringing their political leadership along with them. But even as the city builds out its bike network at a great pace, trying to keep up with the ever increasing rate of cycling, there is something not quite right.[203]

You can tell by looking at a map. On it, city streets that are designated as bicycle routes are marked with a colored line. You can bike on any street in the city—but these ones are called out as recommended and convenient routes. The problem comes once you get onto the actual street. The routes on the map aren't all that great to bike on, at least not all of them. Some routes have bike lanes, which are okay when you're careful. Many are quiet neighborhood streets with low speed limits and good crossings at busier roads. But some of these recommended bike routes are the busier roads themselves, with no concession to two wheeled travelers but a painted sharrow marking in the lane, fading rapidly as car traffic rushes across it at 35 miles per hour.

Sharrows—the word is an amalgamation of "shared lane" and "arrow"—are essentially a five-foot long picture of a bicycle with a double chevron atop it, pointing the way forward. They do not have any legal impact on how people use the road. They are simply there to remind people in cars to look out for bicycles, and to remind people on bicycles that they have every right to be there.

Sharrows have been around for a while, but they started spreading through the streets of major cities in the last few years, after they were endorsed by the federal government. They can be done well, when used clearly and consistently.[204] But many cities, like Seattle, use them somewhat indiscriminately and confusingly. You can be riding along on a nice, quiet street, following the sharrows, and suddenly find yourself being honked at on a fast, narrow road. Locals learn and use the routes they like, but a tourist perusing Seattle's bike map no longer has a clear way to know which routes will be mellow and which will be fast.

The reason for the proliferation of sharrows is that they are politically easy. They cost appealingly little—less than three hundred dollars per marking. More to the point, they do not require planners or politicians to reduce the space used for cars. As for their effectiveness as traffic markings, a few studies have been done; the conclusion is that cyclists are slightly safer when sharrows are present than when they are not, but that the real benefit comes from reducing conflicts between moving and parked cars. But at their best, sharrows are essentially a marketing tool: they proclaim the peaceful coexistence of bicycles and cars without either enforcing that peace or making it easier.

It's no accident that sharrows are so popular in the U.S. The idea that streets are for cars is deeply ingrained here. Leave your home by any other means—cycling or walking, by skateboard or rollerblades, on horseback or via transit—and you're expected to make way for cars, no matter what limited rights the law might give you. Try to make any physical changes on the street that might inconvenience someone while driving, and you'll likely have a raging fight on your hands—and not just from frustrated drivers.

We have a lot of information about the economic and safety impacts of driving and the benefits of bicycling. So why are symbolic sharrows flourishing while more effective forms of bicycle infrastructure languish? Unfortunately, bicycle advocates in the U.S. have often shared, and even added their voices to the chorus that roads are meant for cars and cyclists must fend for themselves or get out of the way.

To understand this, a little history is needed. Back in the 1960s and '70s, bicycle movements grew strong in both in the U.S. and the Netherlands. In both countries, cycling had once been common, but had become more or less equally rare. Suburban expansion was in full swing, cars had become the norm, and air quality was horrible. But then, in the 1970s, fuel shortages curtailed our driving. Freeways were still being built, but the anti-freeway movement was celebrating some successes, and the spirit of social movements at the time gave people pause about what all that driving had wrought.

In the Netherlands, the bicycle movement began in the streets, with citizen activists demanding an end to the free rein of automobility, with cries of "Stop the Child Murder."[205] Activists persisted, and won their point. Their momentum multiplied and reached the highest levels of power. Laws and infrastructure were reworked to make bicycles an attractive choice. As a result, bicycling became mainstream, as it had been once before, unremarkable, a normal way to get around from childhood to old age, with safe, comfortable, convenient facilities provided in every town and city as a matter of course.

In the U.S., we got off to a good start. People started to ride on their own initiative, organizations formed, and some trails and bike lanes were built. Things really took off in places that heavily invested in bike infrastructure networks, like Davis, California and Eugene and Corvallis, Oregon—three of the top bicycle cities in the nation to this day. Popular bicycling movements were more limited here. Residents of New York City rallied for a car-free Manhattan, but for the most part organized street activism on bicycles didn't take off.

A bicycle renaissance like the one occurring in Amsterdam wasn't meant to be, at least not yet. Bicycling had been normal and widespread prior to the rise of the car, and among children up through the 1950s. But we didn't seize the moment in the 1970s. Instead, as baby boomers grew up and the economy rebounded in the late 1980s, bicycling declined to nearly nothing.

A new brand of American bicycle advocacy did come out of this tumultuous era. In 1976, one of the most influential books about cycling ever published came out: John Forester's *Effective Cycling*. In the book, and in every forum possible in the nearly 40 years since its release, Forester advocates cuttingly against bicycle lanes and any other alterations of the roadway intended to attract or protect two-wheeled users. Instead, he claims, the only acceptable way to promote bicycling is to educate cyclists to share the roads with car traffic. "Cyclists fare best when they act and are treated as drivers of vehicles" is his infamous rallying cry. What's more, he insists, anyone who cannot or is unwilling to share the road with traffic, even on 45 mile per hour arterials, has no business riding a bike.

To be sure, on roads that are mostly used by people in cars, defensive cycling skills are a bonus, and bicycle education programs do good work bolstering the skills and confidence of new riders. But Forester and followers of his "vehicular cycling" philosophy take it too far, aggressively lobbying against efforts to make roads more bike friendly. In this, they have been all too effective, successfully convincing city governments throughout the U.S. and Canada that "the bicycle advocates" think that bike infrastructure is dangerous and a waste of money.

It's a message that goes down easily for non-bicycling politicians with tight budgets. As a result, just one or two vocal vehicularists can stymie an entire city's progress on bicycling, no matter how many others may want or need the option to ride. And though the influence of the movement is fading as its most strident proponents age out, it's still winning battles. In recent years, much-needed bike access projects in Ottawa, Canada and Saint Louis, Missouri have been canceled, even as a new freeway bypass is being built through the heart of the latter city.

The orthodoxy of vehicular cycling has taken its economic toll. While the cycling movement of the Netherlands laid the groundwork for what would become the safest streets for bicycling in one of the most prosperous countries of the world, U.S. advocates sought grants to provide intensive education to nervous would-be bicycle commuters while investment in new roads and suburbs ballooned apace. Now, any child or elderly person, rich or poor, any parent rolling slowly with heavy cargo of kids and groceries, can conveniently and cheaply travel under their own power anywhere in the Netherlands. In the U.S., cycling has until very recently remained the last resort of the poor and the preserve of well-to-do hobbyists seeking an adrenaline rush.

Forty years later, we are just starting to make the changes the Dutch made in the seventies. Bicycle advocacy in the U.S. is still shaking off the last vestiges of its ugly bout with vehicularism. Sharrows are a clear reminder of that history—the fundamental notion that if cyclists are going to use the roads, we must play by the rules created for automobiles or bear the consequences.[206] They represent the internal struggles within our bicycle movements. And they point the way to how far we have left to go.

In just a few more decades, if we follow the course we have finally set out upon in earnest, bicycling in our country could become as mundane and widespread as it is in Amsterdam—or more so. For the sake of our economy, health, equity, and sanity, I hope that it does.

In the meantime, we have plenty of roadblocks to overcome.

There's a wonderful photo on the Internet of Senator Chuck Schumer from New York, pedaling down a protected bike lane in Brooklyn, smiling.[207]

In other circumstances, the photo might be most notable as a welcome proof that a powerful U.S. lawmaker rides a bicycle on a regular basis. But in this case, the picture is laugh-out-loud amazing because of just how hard Schumer's family fought the addition of that very lane.

The lane in question is on Prospect Park West, the street on which Schumer's family lives in the well-heeled Park Slope neighborhood of Brooklyn. It is what is known as a protected bike lane, or cycle track. There are different ways to build these lanes; this one was painted bright green and divided to accommodate two directions of bicycle traffic on one side of the busy, one-way street. Road width from an existing traffic lane was repurposed for bicycles while the row of parked cars, along with a buffer for opening car doors, was moved to protect the cyclists from traffic. It's an elegant solution to a major gap in the city's bicycle network.

The lane was installed in June, 2010, with the overwhelming support of local residents. When it was built, it unleashed a tremendous latent demand and was quickly filled with locals as well as people passing through from other parts of New York. A study before and after the bike lane went in found a 61% reduction in speeding and dramatically improved safety at intersections.[208] The street went from being essentially a highway to a welcoming boulevard that was safer for drivers as well.

Yet shortly after the ribbon was cut, flyers started appearing in the neighborhood. "Upset about the 'new' PPW?" they read. "Afraid to stop or even open your car door? Can't park? Difficulties crossing the street? The danger, congestion, and noise caused by the addition of the bike lanes must be stopped! YOU can make it happen!"

The flyers came from a small, well-connected group of residents who included both Schumer's daughter and his wife, Iris Weinshall. Until three years before, Weinshall had been New York City's transportation commissioner. Her replacement, Janette Sadik-Khan, immediately set about undoing the cars-first policies of Weinshall and other commissioners before her. The city was rapidly being transformed by a network of bike lanes, including this latest, right outside Weinshall's front door.

Bike lanes had been erased in the city before at the quiet behest of politically astute elites. Weinshall's group did their utmost to repeat the same trick, using their connections in a full court press to gain access to the city council and place anti-bicycle lane stories in the news, and even filing a lawsuit, which was quickly thrown out. Schumer himself refused to publicly comment on the lane, but public request documents showed that he had, in private, willingly lent his influence to open doors for the group of opponents.

A coalition of neighbors and safe streets advocates poured their resources into fighting back, with much of the battle happening in the media. The threat ultimately did not succeed: the bike lane stayed.

And then, nearly two years after the lane was built, and several months after the furor died down, that photograph surfaced: the Senator, pedaling comfortably along the bike lane he had nearly helped to remove, smiling.

• • •

Good bicycle infrastructure can completely change a city. I've witnessed this firsthand in the east coast cities where I spent the first half of my life— New Haven, New York, and Washington, DC.

In my teens and early twenties, none of these cities had any bicycle infrastructure to speak of. When you rode, you were on your own, taking your chances, ignored, or yelled at.

In New Haven, I rode everywhere, but whenever I left the grid of my neighborhood, I took to the sidewalk. One Friday, as I rode downtown on the sidewalk through the park on my way home from work, there was a cluster of people on bicycles standing around. One of them was Matt Feiner, the guy who worked on my bike at the local shop. "Come join us!" he said. Of course I did.

This was my first Critical Mass, and there were nine of us. We took to the asphalt, zooming and swooping through the rush hour streets that I didn't dare ride on by myself. Even our small numbers were enough to carve out a safe space, and it left me hungry for more.

A year later, my partner and I loaded our bikes into his pickup truck and drove to New York together. I was not experienced at riding in traffic, and that day in Manhattan was unforgettable. As we took our bikes out of the truck, a fashionably-dressed girl on the curb next to us flagged down and climbed into a cab. She personified my dream of living in New York, and I longed to be like her. We rode straight to a lunch place, and as we locked our bikes to a pole outside, a cab screeched to a halt beside us and the same girl emerged. We had been faster, I thought, marveling at everything. I rode on a roller coaster of adrenaline all day, taking the lane on wide, fast, one-way streets like Eighth Avenue, pedaling furiously in high gear, dodging trucks and swerving around the taxis that sped around us. I loved the pure thrill of relying on my balance, wits, and luck to stay alive, but it also terrified and drained me. That night when I got in bed, I started shaking and couldn't stop, finally falling into a troubled sleep early in the morning.

Nearly a decade later, in 2009, I visited New York again, just for an afternoon. With some trepidation, I set off to ride around downtown during the daytime. It was a changed city. The streets were full of bicycles. Eighth Avenue had a protected bike lane and I cruised down it at a leisurely pace, able to give equal attention to staying upright and scanning passing businesses for a spot to stop for lunch. Even having to occasionally merge into car traffic to avoid a parked delivery truck or swerve around a wrong-way delivery cyclist couldn't bring back a shadow of that hectic, traumatic ride I'd undertaken at 22.

That night I hefted my folding bike onto a Chinatown bus to Washington, DC. to go to a conference and visit my sister. I stayed there for a week, taking a guided tour of the city's handful of new bike lanes and paths, enjoying a scenic ride down along the Anacostia River and out to the Nationals stadium, where there was ample bike parking. But the rest of the time, riding between places I actually needed to go in the city, I was transported right back to the bad old days. I'd gotten my sister a bike for Christmas the year before, and was eager to explore the city with her, but she refused. A few months before, an intern her age, Alice Swanson, had been hit by a truck and killed right along what would be my sister's commute in Dupont Circle. My sister and her friends all agreed that bicycling in DC was too dangerous to seriously consider. I had to agree, but I kept riding, gritting my teeth and staying sharp. In the past decade, I had become a skilled and confident rider, but Portland had spoiled me—I could no longer enjoy the thrill of fear, and every ride down a busy avenue felt like something to be survived and endured rather than relished.

Later, DC had its own transformational moment. When I was next there in early 2013, a bicycle network had sprung up that outshone anything I'd imagined. In less than four years, much of the city had actually become an easy and even pleasant place to bike. Good routes were clearly marked, busier streets had protected lanes, and the bike-share system ensured that cyclists were everywhere and drivers knew how to handle that. Even walking around the city felt less like courting death than it had before.

And full circle, back to New Haven—the bike transformation there is happening as well, and in as dreamily and uncontentious a way as I've ever seen. The year I moved away, Matt Feiner opened his own bike shop and it became the hub of the city's growing bicycle movement. The ranks of Critical Mass swelled to hundreds of riders. Feiner also cofounded the advocacy group Elm City Cycling, which enjoys the backing of local media, the police, the mayor and city council, and powerful Yale University. All these forces have enthusiastically embraced bicycling as a matter of course, encouraging Critical Mass and adding to the roster of regular events, slowly putting in bike lanes and calming streets, and even launching a small bike-share system. A rail trail now connects the northern suburbs with the center of downtown. Dozens of local families have begun carrying their kids around on cargo bicycles, perhaps the surest sign yet that my former home is becoming a place that young people like I used to be can get around on two wheels without taking to the sidewalks.

The biggest change I noticed, though, was the smiles. The New Haven I remember was depressed, glum, with groggy punk music blaring out of every retail establishment. Now, people smile as they bike past you on the street. At least, this was my idle observation—and at least one researcher has found a statistically significant overlap between cities that rank high for happiness and the ones that rank the most bicycle-friendly.[209] My old town hasn't hit either list yet, but all signs show that there's hope.

The thing is, this stuff works. When you make streets inviting, convenient, and comfortable for bicycling, people come ride on them in droves. Just two years after it was built, the Prospect Park West lane had seen a 190% increase in riders on weekdays, a third of them children.[210] New York City added 200 miles to its bikeway network between 2007 and 2012. The number of people cycling throughout the city doubled during that time.

The vast majority of people, whether or not they ride a bicycle, enjoy the results—the calmer traffic, the boost for existing local retail business, and the enticement to new ones to take advantage of all the new eyes on the street. People who do ride bikes tend to go out of their way to use good bike streets, and people who don't ride at all, or very much, suddenly turn up on the statistical radar in bike counts and surveys. A little bit of bike infrastructure, even badly-designed, does a substantial amount of good. A systematic and well-designed approach works like magic.

Different streets call for different measures. Protected bike lanes that may be necessary on the busiest, fastest roads can be overkill on smaller, mellower streets. In all cases of bicycle infrastructure, a significant, though hard-to-measure, amount of the positive effects seem to come not just from separating bicycles from cars but also from people walking. The effects of simply slowing down the cars may be equally significant. But at the end of the day, you cannot have a truly bikeable city, where any person will feel comfortable riding, unless you change the streets to make a space for bikes. The fact that everyone benefits, pedestrians and drivers as well, is the icing on the cake.

• • •

Imagine if Critical Mass raised money to pay the police to escort the ride and hundreds of people showed up, including whole families—and everyone was singing and chanting and having a grand time—and it happened twice a week.

That's how it is in Oaxaca, Mexico. The rides are called Paseo de Todos—the ride for everyone—and they happen on most Wednesday and Friday nights. The one I went on happened to be the last Friday in September 2012, the twentieth anniversary of that first Critical Mass in San Francisco. I had intended to be in San Francisco that night for the anniversary ride, but followed the diaspora instead to Oaxaca for the Fifth National Urban Cycling Conference.

Over a thousand people of all ages swerved their bikes jubilantly around bus-sized potholes, miscellaneous piles of debris, double-parked cars, and each other. Someone passed out little plastic whistles and their shrill sound was the backdrop for constant chants. "This one means 'Less cars, more dancing!'" explained the woman next to me at the start. The next chant, "Arriba la bici!" needed no translation.

Oaxaca is a luminous city, a haven for artists in the mountains of southern Mexico. It is not particularly bike friendly. The narrow streets of downtown are paved with cobblestones and they are all one-way. They are loosely arranged into three lanes: one for parking (sometimes part of this is blocked off and reserved for a private business to use), one for double parking, and one for barreling through at top speed. In Mexico, I was told, you do not always need to take a test to get a driver's license. Outside downtown, fast arterials are filled with buses and taxis.

The streets aren't particularly friendly no matter how you're traveling, but absolutely no accommodations are made for cycling. A new friend brought me to her favorite market and introduced me to the proprietors of the coffee cart as a visiting bicycle advocate. They immediately started listing off people they were close to who have died while bicycling.

But Oaxaca has one terrific advantage when it comes to bikes—a parade culture. Almost any night of the week, year-round, you're guaranteed to happen upon a walking or dancing procession, complete with giant puppets and a brass band, delighting everyone but surprising only the tourists. And twice a week, hundreds of families turn out to ride together, creating a safe space on the otherwise car-infested streets.

In Tijuana, a large city close to the U.S. border, the streets are just as unfriendly to cyclists most of the time. There, too, a big, freewheeling ride provides a space of safety and belonging on the road for a diverse cross-section of families on bicycles—and this one is four times a week. It's organized by the Otay Paradise Bicycle Club, so named, one of the organizers explained to me, because Tijuana is on the Otay Mesa, and, when it's filled with bicycles, it's paradise on earth. The rides are officially leaderless, but a handful of the more passionate participants have stepped up to the opportunity for responsibility. Now, they want to take things to the next level and go after political support and permanent infrastructure that's friendly to cycling.

On the final day of the conference, we created some infrastructure ourselves—we painted a bike lane along four blocks of a downtown street. The conference organizers had acquired a permit for this—Oaxaca is a city of artists, and the permit was not for transportation infrastructure, but for a piece of temporary public art. As the paint dried on each block and we moved onto the next, laying down stencils and daubing at the street with paint brushes, car traffic continued to flow, some drivers staying outside the new, wide lane, others continuing as though it wasn't even there. A few hours later the nightly thunderstorm washed it away.

"People in Mexico do not like to change," a young person who works for the government told me. What does it take, then, I asked, thinking about the country's history of revolution. "If the politicians do something new, then the people will decide to do it too," she said. Perhaps she was thinking of Mexico City where recent mayors have been tackling the city's gridlock and smog by instituting a bike-share program, bus rapid transit, and other driving reduction strategies.

Another new friend had a different perspective. "If it is seen as being for families," she suggested, then bicycling could take hold in Mexico.

It's hard not to believe that change is possible when you're riding through city streets at night surrounded by hundreds of smiling families, and spend the next day in a courtyard packed with several hundred of the most determined and spirited advocates you've ever met.

The energy at the conference was palpable—everyone there had the determination of a pioneer, and felt they had a mandate. And it was democratic—the founders of Bicired, a new national advocacy organization, and delegates from Institute for Transportation and Development Policy, an influential international policy center based in Mexico City, mixed freely with student activists, artists, journalists, and ride organizers. The experience reminded me of the Los Angeles Bicycle Summit in 2009, where there was a sense that a movement that had been building slowly for a long time was suddenly coming together into a shared vision. From the packed improvised bike corral in front of the conference building, the future of bicycling in Mexico looked wide open.

So perhaps it's an advantage, at this point in time, that the distance between today's Mexican cities and bicycle paradise is being bridged with very little help from politicians. By the time the electeds catch on, there will already be a popular movement far more powerful and lasting than anything a half-hearted bureaucratic campaign could create.

Similarly, when I visited Spokane, Washington in 2010, it didn't feel very bikeable. The city has its Centennial Trail, a gorgeous bike path along the river. But downtown, the streets were wide, one-way thoroughfares populated by speeding cars. Half of the streets downtown had been torn up and were under construction, and we were told that when they were repaved there would be bike lanes.

To get to the north part of town, where we were staying, we had to take what was essentially a highway. Six lanes wide, it was signed at 35 mph, but nobody was going that slowly except when the cars were bunched up at a light. There was no sidewalk, no bike lane, no shoulder, and no trees next to the road—they had all been cut way back to improve driver sight lines, a classic road safety improvement that makes roads faster, harder to cross, and ultimately less safe.

Spokane had a vibrant bicycle community, though, that had sprung up in just the past three years. A thriving community bike project, Pedals2People was one hub. Critical Mass was another. Spokane was going through a sustainability renaissance, and bicycling was embraced as a part of this. The city is a hub for outdoors enthusiasts, and the mountain bikers and club riders had an interest in improving city streets. Almost a thousand people registered for the first Bike to Work day event in 2008; organizers had aimed for 300. The energy for bikes in the city was palpable, and it seemed like a new ride or organization was forming every month.

One of the most popular of these new players was the F.B.C.— short for Effing Bike Club. Their monthly nighttime ride, the Full Moon Fiasco, was essentially a pub crawl on bikes. Anyone who wanted to turn up rode from bar to bar together. Sometimes there were themed costume rides, sometimes the rides ended in organized parties with games and prizes, and sometimes they'd head to the hills outside of town and ride around dirt roads all night. The club began in St Louis, Missouri, and when one of its members, Jeff Everett, moved to Spokane, he started a local chapter. At the first ride, only he and his wife showed up. It grew from there until over a hundred people were coming out every full moon, year-round. Some rides, in the summer, had twice that number. Once the bar they ended at ran out of beer.

They had a ride the night we were there. While we were waiting for it to start, I chatted with an advocate from the local Complete Streets nonprofit. Her campaign had been a nonstarter at City Hall for a long time, she said. There were a couple of city commissioners who rode bikes, but the rest just didn't get it. Why build bike lanes when so few people rode bikes in Spokane already? And nobody ever would ride in very great numbers, they believed, especially not at night or in the winter. It was the defiantly apolitical F.B.C. rides that turned the tide, she told me. Hundreds of people on bikes, at night, in frosty January? And in their street clothes, no less, and providing brisk trade for local businesses. That was the proof that was needed. And so Spokane got its bike lanes—just stripes of paint on a busy road, nothing revolutionary, but a beginning, until the next level of citizen demand becomes unavoidably clear.

Take the example of Portland. Most of our bicycle infrastructure was built in the 1990s, during the era of Critical Mass, and by some accounts, in response to it. If you measure only commuters, we had low ridership at that time, quite a bit less than cities like Minneapolis or Seattle. Between 2001 and 2010s, we added only 30 miles of bike lanes, but our rate of bike commuting increased by six times. Portland's rise to bicycle fame and fortune owes as much to the city's human infrastructure as to the paint and concrete type.

On the other hand, could there have been a bicycle boom in the 2000s if the way had not been paved, so to speak, in the 1990s, or even in the 1970s before it, when citizen activists stopped the build out of the city's freeway network and an innovative urban growth boundary slowed its outward sprawl? Many cities are struggling to keep up with the demand for bike lanes; and it's possible that Portland's ridership was able to grow so fast, once the movement hit, because we already had enticing places for people to ride. Our early investment was prescient.

There is no master recipe for building a bicycle friendly city. The places where bicycling catches on all seem to have their own unique combination of top-down leadership and grassroots movements. The two forces rely on each other, and the push and pull and friction between them is what drives change.

It's always easier to change nothing, or to lay down a few sharrows and walk away. It's harder to erase bike infrastructure once it's been put in, but it can be done with a little political maneuvering and a few hours with a pavement grinder. No matter how bicycle-friendly a politician or transportation bureau seems, they can only do their job if they know the people have their backs—or are holding their feet to the fire.

Cars didn't become mainstream because people just decided to start driving one day, or because charismatic leaders and lobbyists deemed that it would be so. There was serious organization, by advocates but also on a grassroots level—motoring clubs, drag races, groups of friends that went on motor outings. Many of these organizations began for pleasure and fun, not for politics. But they were at least as, if not more, influential than advocates and politicians in creating a culture of normalcy, inevitability, and cultural identification around driving.

We are waking up to the urgency of our transportation problems. Alone, without a community to work with and ride with, we can educate ourselves well enough to get by, but have little hope of real change. For change to come, we need to work together, building communities, cultures, movements, and political will.

The need for a popular bicycling movement will recede as cycling becomes more mainstream. When bicycling no longer feels like an adrenaline rush, a radical act, or a dangerous sport requiring intensive education, we'll no longer need Critical Mass or a *ciclovía*.

We aren't there yet. But we're getting there with remarkable speed. Cities that have found that magic combination of public determination and political verve are finding it takes only two or three years for cycling to become an accepted feature of their landscape. And history on the other side of the Atlantic shows us that it only takes a decade or two before it's so normal that we forget we ever needed to take to the streets and speak up.

Rethinking The Future

When two sections of the I-5 bridge over the Skagit River collapsed north of Seattle in May, 2013, the disaster brought immediate attention to the crumbling state of the Interstate system, particularly bridges.

News coverage hammered home the grim facts: Eleven percent of bridges in the nation, including a quarter of the bridges in Washington State, are structurally deficient.

But the Skagit River Bridge was not one of them. The part of the story that never got more than a passing mention in the media is that the bridge did not fall as a result of its structural defects, unless it is a defect to have been built in another era. The cause of the collapse was a truck that struck the bridge's overhead structure several times. The truck was too large for the bridge, taller than the maximum height indicated for crossing and larger than the bridge's designers, half a century earlier, had likely ever imagined a truck could be. At the time of the collapse, the truck was in service delivering heavy oil-drilling equipment from the Port of Vancouver, Washington to the Alberta Tar Sands oil fields. The equipment was housed in large containers for the trip, and it is one of these empty containers that struck the bridge struts on the southbound trip.[211]

Such equipment is not normally carried on freeways. In fact, the route that the trucking company had originally planned to use was through the Montana wilderness. Communities along this route had protested the use of their rural highways, complaining of the ecological devastation and the damage to a tourism and hunting-based economy that would result. In a rare turn of events, the protests were successful, and the oil-drilling equipment was rerouted onto the I-5 freeway. Unlike rural roads, freeways are built to withstand heavy loads, and extra large traffic is less disruptive, though it still causes substantial wear and tear that needs to be eventually repaired at taxpayer expense.[212] But no roads at all have been built to haul trucks of this size and weight, not even the Interstate.

Our energy crisis is in every way a transportation crisis. And to a degree, so is the climate crisis posed by the global warming effects of that energy use.

Our auto-based transportation system relies not only on a myth of endless growth—and with it the expansion of resource-hungry homes and industries—it relies on an endless supply of fuel to keep itself operating.

We in the United States consume 22% of the world's oil.[213] The transportation sector accounts for more than two thirds of this oil, mostly in the form of gasoline.

Forty percent of that gas goes directly into the fuel tanks of our cars. That's 377 million gallons every single day—a bit more than a gallon per U.S. resident, including the 1/3 of us who don't have driver's licenses. That's more than the daily amount of water most of us drink.

We're paying for it on a number of levels, though we pay less than we tend to think we do. Our price at the pump, no matter how high it gets, always stays cheaper than in Europe, where drivers currently shell out between $7 to $10 per gallon.

The real price of the gas we use every day is much higher. If we paid the true price of our fuel, our gas would cost $7 to $15 per gallon at the pump, depending on the subsidies and other externalities considered.

Many of these externalized costs are in the form of millions of dollars in tax breaks each year to the oil industry, funding every step from production to import. These companies enjoy some of the highest annual profits of any business in the country, and we all pay for them to keep doing such booming business—$78 billion in subsidies was paid out between 2002 and 2008 alone. It's worth noting that in the same time, $29 billion was dedicated to subsidizing renewable fuel, but half of that went to corn—which aside from producing equally-dirty, hard-to-use fuel at a near loss in net energy, is wreaking havoc with our agricultural economy and landscape. More investment in true renewables makes sense, and there is some exciting innovation out there (deriving fuel cleanly from trash, anyone?). But nothing has been found that can fulfill our current levels of energy use. From an energy policy perspective, we should be investing instead in measures that reduce our demand for energy. Much smaller investments in bicycle infrastructure, for instance, are having a far greater impact on our energy footprint.

As things stand currently, road expansion and sprawl development can also be seen as a major subsidy for the oil industry. Policies that direct public money towards paving new roads, expanding utilities, and giving tax breaks to exurban developers constrain our transportation options. By doing so, they ensure an ever-increasing consumer demand for gasoline.

The freight industry, and the companies it serves, are among those who benefit the most from these subsidies. Trucks, which use nearly four times as much fuel as rail to move a ton of goods coast to coast, represent as well as anything the fragility and scale of the economy we have come to depend on.

One of the largest external costs of our fuel use is war. The exact amount spent on overseas military protection of oil reserves is hotly debated, but conceivably dwarfs all of the rest of the costs discussed in this book. For this reason alone, many Americans, on the left and the right, are eager to be free of foreign fuel.

As with our other transportation problems, we are trying to solve our energy problems on the supply side, by finding more North American energy sources. The quest for fossil fuel continues, and we are finding it. This gas, siphoned from the earth through a process called hydraulic fracturing or fracking, has brought much-needed prosperity to parts of the middle of the country. At the same time it has proven extraordinarily problematic. The resulting wealth is highly concentrated and unevenly distributed, and much of it leaves the areas from which the oil was extracted. Locals benefit in some ways, but also have to contend with housing shortages, rent increases, hazards from increased truck traffic, hazardous air pollution, and the destruction of water supplies. The latter has the potential to damage the health of anyone who drinks or bathes in groundwater, and also the livelihoods of local business owners, like ranchers, who depend on good water. As with the economic benefits of new oil, these external costs are not distributed evenly.

And then there are far reaching effects—like the Skagit River Bridge collapse. Aside from the cost of repairing and ultimately replacing the bridge, which is being covered by the federal government, the collapse was a blow to all levels of the economy along the northern section of I-5. While the bridge was out for a month, everyone felt the impact, from small retail businesses who were cut off from customers to contractors and commuters who needed to spend the extra time—and money on fuel—to get where they needed to go. This one event is a microcosm of the impact of this recent growth of domestic fuel extraction. For a few, it's hugely enriching; for the many who are affected by it, results are mixed.

This becomes most clear in the event of an environmental disaster. In 2010, the Deepwater Horizon oil rig exploded and sank while it was drilling for oil in the Gulf of Mexico. Before the well it was drilling could be capped, nearly 5 million barrels worth of oil poured into the Gulf, devastating ecosystems and livelihoods along the coast. The years-long cleanup process is costing the companies responsible millions of dollars—which happen to be tax-deductible. The wealth from drilling for oil and the fact that our economy is based on the energy it provides are indisputable. But the costs at every level may more than outweigh it.

And then there is the cost of emissions. Every second, the transportation sector in the U.S. burns through 6,300 gallons of oil. Our transportation alone produces more carbon emissions each year than the total pollution from all sectors produced by any other country except China. The toll of this pollution on our personal health is devastating, but its longer term effects are proving to be far more dangerous.

One of the clearest metrics of climate change (or, as it used to be called, global warming) is the amount of carbon dioxide in the atmosphere. Carbon dioxide is necessary to sustain life—in simple terms, we breathe in oxygen and exhale carbon, and plants, in turn, process carbon and convert it to oxygen. The standard balance for much of the history of the inhabited earth has been 275 parts per million (ppm) of carbon in the part of the atmosphere that we breathe. Two hundred years ago, during the industrial revolution, we began to burn massive quantities of coal and gas, and the level of carbon began to climb. It has risen increasingly fast in recent years as we burn more fuel and release more carbon emissions.

The upper limit at which scientists believe the planet can sustain life as we know it is 350ppm of carbon in the atmosphere. We recently passed the 400ppm mark, with levels growing by about 2ppm each year.[216]

The result? Warmer air, melting glaciers, rising sea levels, and destructive weather events. It isn't just the atmosphere that absorbs carbon—the ocean does as well, resulting in higher acidity and the destruction of what is essentially the foundation of the planetary food chain. Mosquitos thrive in a warmer, wetter world, and the diseases they carry have become epidemic again. It's a bad scene.

The effects of a warming world have until recently been felt the most keenly in the so-called Global South. The developed world has been slow to realize and react, though it has also been the source of the bulk of the world's carbon emissions. A series of high profile natural disasters in the last several years that are thought to be related to rising sea levels and shifting storm patterns have made the urgency of global warming far more difficult to avoid.

The question remains: What do we do? Many dire warnings come paired with uninspiring suggestions, like changing our lightbulbs, recycling, and making sure our car tires are adequately inflated. As we wait in vain for the world's leaders to sort it out from the top down, it's becoming increasingly obvious that most of us are hungry to do more ourselves.

It turns out that transportation is one of the best opportunities we have to take action. A 2010 NASA study pinpointed motor vehicles—private cars and freight trucks—as the most-effective first line of attack for tackling the problem of carbon emissions.[214]

Motor vehicles may not, in themselves, be the worst offenders in global warming. Industry and shipping sectors emit more carbon overall, which has a warming effect on the atmosphere, but they also emit aerosols or sulfates. Aerosols are terrible for the health of people who breathe them, but they also have a cooling effect on the atmosphere, masking their contribution to global warming at least in the short term. Because automobiles do not emit aerosols, the NASA scientists found, they are disproportionately responsible for short term global warming effects. Instead of focusing on regulating specific chemicals, the scientists suggested, it would be more practical and effective to focus on the net impacts of specific economic sectors—in this case transportation.

Where does this lead us?

When we talk about reducing transportation emissions, the conversation tends to solely be about cars and fuel. Efforts to invent and promote electric and hybrid cars have enjoyed some success, and have proven the latent market demand for lower-emission personal transportation. These vehicles pollute less, but they still require roads and parking spaces, are susceptible to crashes, and contribute to a dispersed and unhealthy landscape. And they are far from energy-neutral.

The world currently burns enough fuel to release about 31 gigatons—a gigaton is one billion tons—of carbon into the atmosphere every year.[215] The United States contributes more than 7 of those gigatons, with transportation contributing to nearly a third of that amount.

Our current bicycle infrastructure investments in the United States alone save 12 million tons of carbon emissions every year, by one estimate. Moderate investment in the future could save 23 million tons a year, and more substantial investment could save as much as 91 million tons a year. It's a small piece of the puzzle, not insignificant but not world-saving on its own, either—though it's certainly one of the most cost-effective climate remedies out there.

What are bicycles good for, then?

Peak oil is old hat, and perhaps has been for several decades. And it is no longer necessary to await apocalyptic disaster as major world cities are shattered by earthquakes and flooded by rising tides and increasingly large storms.

The rising price of gas, the health care crisis, and the terrible economy have constituted a true disaster for many households in recent years. Many have been responding, whether out of optimism or pure, desperate necessity, by taking up bicycling. The fact that cycling has not declined again as the price of gas drops shows that people are finding that it works for us, and even that we prefer it.

In larger scale disasters, bicycles are also proving to be valuable resources. After a hurricane, a tornado, or a flood, the streets tend to be clogged with debris, fuel is unavailable, cars are out of commission, and resources are strained. A bicycle with tough, knobby tires is often the only way to get around the city. These are times when the latent demand for bicycling makes itself known.

In New York City after Hurricane Sandy, power was out, streets were blocked, and transit wasn't running. Bicycle sales and repairs skyrocketed. Shops couldn't keep bikes on the shelves, and mechanics worked double shifts getting people's bicycles up and running. Bicycling levels anecdotally stayed high after the subway system became available again and roads opened. In other disasters, such as after the Kobe earthquake in 1995 in Japan, bicycles were the only way first responders could arrive from outside the city.

During an evacuation, in fact, cars often are the disaster. Hurricane Rita did minimal damage to Houston, but the freeways away from the city were clogged for days with cars which had broken down, run out of gas, or been involved in crashes.

We're all in crisis these days, or in the midst of multiple crises, though we experience and respond to them in different ways. The bicycle isn't a silver bullet that will solve any of them on its own—not health, not loneliness, not fear, not global catastrophe, not the economy. It's easy to long for a single solution to all our problems, technological or otherwise, but no such thing exists. For good or for ill, it seems unlikely that we'll come through the next decade without serious shifts in how we see and live in the world, and nothing will change that, either.

Whatever our challenges, we're better able to face them when we are relatively fit, healthy, happy, prosperous, confident, and on confidently equal footing with each other, and able to forge strong connections within and between communities. We need these things desperately, and an increasing number of communities are turning to the bicycle for them, with some success.

The bicycle is, at this moment in history, the rare tool that reminds us that we have the power to help ourselves and each other in exactly the ways that will allow us to face the worst of the disasters we find ourselves in.

What the bicycle can do—if we choose to use it this way—is help us survive and move beyond these things ourselves, to the best of our capabilities. The bicycle may not be able to save either the economy or the world that we have now. But it is one means by which we may be able to get through whatever comes next with grace and meaning. And it provides us with the opportunity to build ourselves lives, communities, and an economy that we can truly afford for the long run.

Acknowledgments

This book began as an idea when I was writing a regular column on bicycling for **Grist**. My editor there was **Sarah Goodyear**; without her encouragement and sharp editing skills, I would not have gone on to write this book. I also owe a debt of thanks to **Jonathan Maus** at **BikePortland**, who first asked me to write about bicycling.

Several of the sections of this book were worked out and initially published in a much different form on my own blog at **TakingtheLane.com**, at **Grist.org**, on the **Everyday Rider** blog at **Bicycling.com**, and in the form of a much shorter zine, also titled *Bikenomics*.

I'm standing on the shoulders of a number of pioneering researchers. Every time I think of a new and exciting question, I'm bound to discover that **Todd Litman** has already published an exhaustive paper on the topic. Without the quantitative work of **Charles Komanoff, John Pucher, Jennifer Dill, Anne Lusk, Roger Geller, Peter Jacobsen, Kelly Clifton, Thomas Gotschi**, and others, much of what I have written would be pure speculation. Any erroneous readings of their research are my own.

My research was greatly aided by the publications and staff of several livable streets organizations: **Streetsblog, Bikes Belong, Rails to Trails**, the **Alliance of Bicycling and Walking**, and the **League of American Bicyclists.**

Thank you to the many friends and colleagues who have shared inspiration, conversation, food, encouragement, and long emails full of statistics. The second edition benefited greatly from a peer review by **Dr. Adonia Lugo**. Many of the improvements in this edition are the result of her careful feedback. All remaining missteps are entirely my own doing.

Several readers got in touch and offered conversation, clarifying questions, advocacy anecdotes, and photos of their amazing bicycle inventions; I thank you all, this book is better because of you. **Maysa Blay** and **Tati Carvalho** translated the book into Brazilian Portuguese and brought many unclear passages and errant endnotes to my attention. Extra thanks are due to **Tomy Huynh**, who came in as the editor of the second edition, tackling my hasty sentence structure and untangling the endnotes.

This book owes its existence in many ways to **Joe Biel**, who also came up with the title.

The entire staff at **Microcosm**, then and now, have been incredibly supportive and encouraging.

Especial thanks to everyone who has used the book as it was originally intended: as a tool for making communities better.

Last but not least, long live all the friends, strangers, people we met on tour, colleagues, blog commenters, and social media acquaintances who have contributed their data, stories, perspectives, rants, raspberries, ideas, encouragement, and skepticism. This book is dedicated to you.

(Endnotes)

1 According to our host, the longtime loggerheads between fans of the Browns and the Steelers touched every aspect of life and informed every cultural priority. Pittsburgh was, at that time, teetering on the verge of bankruptcy. But in the past several years, savvy community leaders had made the connection between the growth of bicycling and the civic savings that could come from encouraging it and bikes were booming. Pittsburgh was recognized as a Bicycle Friendly Community by the League of American Bicyclists in 2010 (Cleveland did not achieve this status until 2013—it was announced the same month we visited), and the advocacy organization, BikePGH, was named the best in the nation by the Alliance of Biking and Walking in 2011.

2 According to the World Bank, Brazil has the third biggest divide between rich and poor in the world (behind Honduras and Colombia; the United States is 15th. The inclusion of South Africa in 2011 only and Haiti in 2012 only both caused Brazil to drop to fourth place, and it may be that the class divide is far greater in many countries where this sort of economic data is not available). This is measured using the Gini Coefficient scale of income distribution. These numbers are the most recent available, from 2013.

3 Personal communication.

4 Clark's story and background on Detroit Bike & Brunch is from detroitbikebrunch.com and personal communications.

5 T. Litman, "Whose Roads," 2012 (an update of his 2004 research). By Litman's example, an average driver underpays for the road system by $236 every year. A person who only travels by bicycle overpays by $252.

6 Ibid.

7 From Copenhagen City of Cyclists Bicycle Account, 2010. The gains calculated are interesting as well: They include costs, security, comfort, branding, tourism, time, and health.

8 D. Royal and D. Miller-Steiger, "National Survey of Bicyclist and Pedestrian Attitudes and Behavior," NHTSA, 2008.

9 David Leonhardt, "Big Vehicles Stagger Under the Weight of $4 Gas," *New York Times*, June 4, 2008. Leonhardt calculated the cost of a "fully loaded" Ford F-250, which had a $50,000 sticker price, to actually come to $100,000 in total costs over five years, with $30,000 going to gas alone). Meanwhile, a much smaller Ford Focus would cost only $40,000 over that same five-year period. The difference, $60,000, he wrote, was the same as the average U.S. family income that year, meaning that opting for the bigger truck, as many families at that income level did (it sold 165,000 units that year), "is like volunteering for a 20 percent pay cut." His calculations were based on gas staying at $4 per gallon, which it did not, though it has reached that point again several times in the last five years.

10 The numbers here are taken from the AAA's 2013 and 2015 "Your Driving Costs" reports, and include only sedan style cars. The cost of driving an SUV in 2015 was calculated separately at $10,624 with a "large sedan" such as a Toyota Avalon clocking in at about the same cost as an SUV. Also worth noting: These calculations assume that you drive 15,000 miles per year. The average U.S. person drove about 13,500 miles per year in of 2010, according to the FHWA; people between the ages of 20 and 54 drove over 15,000 miles on average. Those numbers are expected to have gone down in subsequent years. Note that this amount is different than the commonly cited statistic of vehicle miles traveled per capita, which is calculated based on population at large rather than just on drivers.

11 All these figures are from the Bureau of Labor Statistics, which polls households, or "consumer units," on their actual spending for the prior year, not to be confused with the AAA's projections, which are for the cost of the particular type of car.

http://www.bls.gov/news.release/cesan.nro.htm.

12 Catherine New, "The 10 Most Expensive U.S. Cities to Park a Car," *Daily Finance*, July 12, 2011.

13 "Income, Expenditures, Poverty, and Wealth: Consumer Expenditures," U.S. Census, Table 688. Households earning under $70,0000 average $5,300 in total transportation spending for the year.

Across all incomes, the average spending on transportation was $7600. Cost for a 4-person family? Over $10,000. The percentage of total expenditure eaten up by transportation became lower among people with higher income. Note that this number is not comparable to the AAA estimates, since it includes the many families that did not buy new vehicles, as well as the smaller number who do not own a car at all. It also does not include depreciation, a major cost of car ownership that is not counted as spending.

14 Researchers have found that people tend to change their driving behavior and choices a full 12 months after gas prices change. Gas prices spiked in 2008, and the car market could have been expected to suffer accordingly in 2009. But that was the year of "Cash for Clunkers," a three billion dollar federal program that subsidized the purchase of new cars. The subsidy was meant to boost domestic auto sales and put safer, more fuel-efficient vehicles on the road. The program was a failure. Most people opted to purchase imported cars, improvements in fuel efficiency were found to be negligible, and a study after the fact found that the public costs of the program exceeded the benefits by $2,000 per vehicle, or over a billion dollars total. A Portland bike shop made national news that year for running their own cash for clunkers program, providing a discount on a new bike in exchange for proof of an old bike being donated to a local community bicycle program.

15 "Impact of Rising Gas Prices on Below-Poverty Commuters," Urban Institute Fact Sheet, September 2008.

16 Noga relayed this story to me in an email interview. Some of the details are adapted from her essay "My Revolution" about the experience of going carfree, which I published in 2012. You can read it on her blog at ibikeubike.com, or another version in Taking the Lane #8: "Childhood." When selling the first car, they dropped their $476 monthly payment and $67 a month in insurance. They had spent $1,014 on gas that year (filling up the tank for $39 every two weeks), which was low because they didn't drive it much. This total does not include maintenance, oil changes, registration, new tires, parking, tickets, or a host of other costs. The remaining car, an import, was being paid off at $546 per month ($6,552 per year), with an interest rate of 4%. Full coverage insurance for two adult drivers with good driving history was 136 per month ($1,632/year). She estimates that they spent $50 to $60 filling up the gas tank every 5 days (about $4,000 per year). Their costs for one car, not including oil changes, maintenance, tires, or registration, added up to $12,184 that year. Three bikes, for the adults and the 11-year old, were $129 each. A kiddie bike for the toddler was $49. Helmets were $30 each. The trailer was $179.

17 T. Litman, "Transportation Cost and Benefit Analysis II—Vehicle Costs," 2011. $308 is a commonly cited annual cost for bicycle commuting. The number is drawn from a 1997 survey of bicycle commuters (Moritz, "Survey of North American Bicycle Commuters, Design and Aggregate Response," 1997) in which the commuters reported spending an average of $308 on new bicycles. Their total reported annual cost was an average of $714, including new bikes, upgrades to existing bikes, and clothing.The average commuter represented in the study was a 39-year-old professional male making $45,000 and owning at least one car. Demographics of bicycle ridership have either shifted significantly since then or are captured differently. Todd Litman has tackled this topic using a standard closer to the AAA's, looking at average vehicle costs rather than consumer spending trends. He puts the annual cost of cycling at $100-$300 per mile, estimating that a transportation bicycle and accessories costs $500-$1000, which annualizes to $50-$100 per year if the bike is ridden for ten years. He adds five to 15 cents per mile in maintenance costs; so $50-$200 if you ride 2,000 miles per year.

18 Van Lenthe et al., in K. Krizek et. al., "Walking and Cycling International Literature Review," Victoria Department of Transportation, 2005.

19 Bureau of Transportation Statistics, 2003.

20 "Service, Efforts, and Accomplishments Survey," Portland City Auditor, 2008.

21 R. Geller, "Four Types of Cyclists." portlandonline.org.

22 D. Meyer, "Perceptions and Possibilities," *League of American Bicyclists*, 2013.

23 National Household Travel Survey; analysis thanks to Richard Masoner. cyclelicio.us.

24 For more details of the art work's history and removal, see Weir, W., "Ghost Lot Being Exhumed," *The Hartford Courant*, Aug 8, 2003.

25 J. Jacobs, *Death and Life of Great American Cities,* 1961.

26 These metrics and analysis were developed by the Center for Neighborhood Technology in 2012. To be deemed affordable, housing should costs 30% or less of residents' total income. Housing and transportation together should take up only 45% of household income. (The highest rate studied was the Miami area, with middle-income households spending 72% of their incomes on housing and transportation combined).

27 "Losing Ground: Housing and Transportation Costs Outpacing Incomes," National Housing Conference and Center for Housing Policy, 2012. Since 2000, transportation and housing costs have increased by 40%, while incomes have only gone up 25%. These average increases are not necessarily experienced equally—for many, these basic costs have gone up at the same time as their income has gone down.

28 "Commuting to Opportunity: The Working Poor and Commuting in the United States," Brookings Institute, 2008. The working poor spend more on both housing and commuting; homeowners living in poverty spend on average 25% of their income on housing while the non-poor spend about 15%. Renters spend 32% of their income on housing while the non-poor spend 20%.

29 From: Pew Research Center, http://www.pewinternet.org/Reports/2013/Teens-and-Tech.aspx. According to research, 93% of teens have access to the Internet.

30 Smiley, et al., "More Inclusive Parks Planning: Park Quality and Preferences for Park Access and Amenities," *Environmental Justice*, 9:1, 2016. The Houston parks studies were reviewed (and afollow-up conducted). Thanks to Dr. Adonia Lugo for bringing up this point in her review of the first edition.

31 J. Terry, "Portland Enjoys a Golden Age of Cycling—A Century Ago," *The Oregonian*, January 22, 2011. The first paved bike path in Oregon was privately funded, with local wheelmen kicking in $1 each to pave the road to The White House, a bar in southwest Portland.

32 The myth that motorists pay for the roads, or even that motorists overpay is still frequently published as fact. The last year that could have been true would have been 1955.

33 Planning estimates from the Arkansas Highway Department, updated July, 2012. This amount refers to center line miles. Costs are higher in mountainous areas. Arkansas has recently passed a ½ cent increase in the sales tax and is going on a massive freeway widening spree with money borrowed against the projected proceeds.

34 "Rails to Trails," *Politifact Oregon*, March 19, 2011. Roger Geller, the City of Portland's bicycle planner, is the originator of this comparison. The replacement value of Portland's entire existing inventory of bicycle infrastructure, including infrastructure used for bicycling but not built solely for the purpose (such as pedestrian bridges) in 2008 was estimated at $52 million—planners rounded it up to $60 million to be on the safe side. On average, cities report planning to spend between $20 and $80 million per mile on urban freeways—a figure that usually ends up being far higher due to the extremely high extra costs of bridges or cloverleafs. The freeway cost is the average cost per mile for a four-lane urban freeway without special restrictions, as reported by a "Rails to Trails" report on nationally collected figures. The real costs may be much higher when taking into account bridges, tunnels, over and underpasses, and various other factors.

35 Angie Schmitt, "Drivers cover just 51 percent of U.S. road spending," *Streetsblog*, January 23, 2013. The road system has been nearly half paid for through subsidies. Compare this with passenger rail—Amtrak is much maligned for requiring public money, but recovers 85% of its operating costs from fares. When you include capital costs, tickets still cover 69% of its spending. For further comparison: Angie Schmitt, "While Amtrak Subsidies Draw Fire From Congress, Aviation Gets a Free Pass," *Streetsblog*, March 12, 2013. Only 70% of the Federal Aviation Administration's budget and less than a third of the Transportation Safety Administration's budget are covered by passenger fees.

36 "Do Roads Pay for Themselves?" USPIRG, 2011. This report uses federal data to show that since 1947 the shortfall between the direct revenue paid by motorists into so-called "user fees" like gas tax, license, and registration and the actual cost of building and maintaining streets, roads, and freeways has been $600 billion (in 2005 dollars). At the time of the report, its authors calculate, user fees paid for 51% of all the nation's road costs, with the rest coming from municipalities' general funds and debt. A decade ago, direct fees made up 61% of road spending. Also: Elana Schor, "New Report: Road Funding From Non-Users Doubled in 25 Years," *Streetsblog*, November 24, 2009. Another study of road subsidies shows that they doubled between 1982 and 2007, from $35 billion to $70 billion a year in 2007 dollars.

37 "Paying Our Way," Executive Summary of the National Surface Transportation Infrastructure Financing Commission, February 2009. What does this gap add up to on a practical policy level? A federal commission to study the problem released grim results in 2009, calling for "dramatic" action. The federal government, the commission estimated, would need to invest $100 billion per year to maintain and improve the nation's freeways; the gas tax at the time was projected to yield $32 billion per year. On all levels of government, the commission further found, $200 billion in transit and road investments a year would be needed, but only a third of that amount could be raised. Forget building new capacity, the report's authors wrote: "policymakers at all levels must use existing revenues simply to attempt to keep pace with the preservation and maintenance of an aging system."

38 Southeastern Wisconsin Regional Planning Commission Planning Report, No. 47. A Regional Freeway Reconstruction System Plan For Southeastern Wisconsin 2005

39 American Society of Civil Engineers, Infrastructure Report Card, 2013.

40 "Repair Priorities," a 2011 report by Smart Growth America and Taxpayers for Common Sense found that between 2004 and 2008, $22 billion dollars, or 57% of state costs were sunk into building new roads—23,300 miles in total. That left less than half the available funding, or a total of $16 billion for repair of the remaining 98.7%, nearly 2 million lane miles, of the nation's state highways. This is despite half of existing state roads being rated in "fair" or "poor" condition two years previously; states that spent the highest percentage of their road budget on new construction during that period saw their overall roadway ratings decline. And the new roads wouldn't be new forever. The report estimates that the new road building has added a cost of $520 million per year overall to states' roadway maintenance budgets, if the roads are repaired when needed and on schedule.

41 The bicycling cities of Europe are famous throughout the world for good reason. Their examples are often taken as comparisons by U.S. bicycle advocates, without taking into account the far greater diversity in landscape and population here. Much of China until the early 21st Century, and several parts of Latin America would be far better comparisons for the issues we face. One thing that wealthy western European cities have, however, that most other places in the world— including the U.S.—do not, is robust data about bicycling and health, which is why I use this example.

42 D. Hemsbrow, "Cycling Infrastructure is Cheaper," *A View from the Cycle Path*, June 27, 2011. Hemsbrow, a British expatriate living in Assen, the Netherlands, keeps a fascinating blog comparing details of his two countries' cycling infrastructure and culture. Interestingly, this particular study also considered a scenario where half of bicycle journeys in the future are made with electric assist bicycles, and predicted an even greater health benefit to the cycling superhighways in that case, since the new technology is expected to lead people to make more longer-distance trips by bicycle.

43 E. Beardsley, "In Bike-Friendly Copenhagen, Highways For Cyclists," NPR, September 1, 2012.

44 J. Greenfield, "Can Chicago Reach 30 Miles of 'Green Lanes' Before the Snow Flies?" *Grid Chicago*, September 27, 2012. Also: J. Greenfield, "Elevating the Conversation: Raised Bike Lanes Are Coming to Chicago," *Streetsblog*, April 8, 2013. Chicago's costs square with what other cities are currently reporting—for instance, new bike lanes in Los Angeles were calculated in 2010 to cost approximately $40,000 per mile. From ladotbikeblog.wordpress.com/bike-lane-projects/ accessed July 18, 2013.

45 The cost of new bike infrastructure tends to be highest when the concept is first introduced, and gets lower over time as less design and engineering labor needs to be put into each one, and the installation process is honed to become more efficient.

46 "Long Beach Master Plan Design and Maintenance," Alta Planning Consulting, September, 2012. Alta Planning estimates the cost of bike lane maintenance to be about $2,000 per mile for repainting aside from maintenance already being done on the road. For multi-use, off-road paths, the most expensive to maintain, they estimate the cost to be $8,500 per mile per year, covering pavement maintenance, sweeping, and trash removal. Places where the bike path must be plowed for snow or regularly swept for broken glass may have higher costs. By comparison, a report on regular road maintenance costs (on average) by the ICMA Knowledge Network, February 10, 2012: "Ninety-four participants reported their road rehabilitation expenditures—per paved lane mile— with an average of $3,867 and a median of $2,894. Eighty-six participants reported street sweeping expenditures per mile swept with an average of $47 and a median of $36." The large difference between mean and median is likely the difference between low-traffic residential streets and major roads with large amounts of traffic and heavy trucks and buses.

47 "Asset Status and Condition Report 2012," Portland Bureau of Transportation, 2012.

48 Just like car-centric projects, bike projects are often paid for with borrowed money, though the amounts at stake are far smaller and more quickly repaid. Recently, several large bicycle infrastructure projects were funded by TIGER stimulus grants. The Chicago infrastructure is funded through neighborhood funding pools as well as through Tax Increment Financing, a popular if controversial method of borrowing money for public works projects against the projected tax revenue increases they stand to bring through the increased real estate value and taxable retail sales hoped for as a result of the project. Chicago has also won a $40 million federal CMAQ (Congestion Mitigation and Air Quality) grant to fund its bicycle infrastructure expansion. Note that this is all borrowed money. I don't know what maintenance plan or budget is in place for the infrastructure, or if a funding mechanism exists for the end of a bike path or parking staple's lifestyle decades down the line. We may be in trouble yet. But based on what we know (and can observe in the more solvent Netherlands, for instance), these investments should produce more than enough savings to cover maintenance and replacement through substantial health benefits and through the tax base benefits of increasing density, mobility, and access. Whether or not the accounting and budgeting process is done in a forward thinking manner is another question, and I think this is an important consideration to add to all infrastructure projects, including bicycling ones.

49 H. Garrett-Peltier, "Pedestrian and Bicycle Infrastructure: A National Study of Employment Impacts," Political Economy Research Institute, June 20, 2011. Jobs are counted compositely. When a project creates 70 jobs, it doesn't mean 70 people will be set on a track to retirement—it might mean that 70 people will work for a year, or more likely that 35 people will work for two years.

50 That year's federal transportation bill included a small pot of "Transportation Enhancements" funding, mostly for bicycle and pedestrian projects that did not otherwise cost enough to qualify for federal transportation grants. Transportation Enhancements funding has been increased, decreased, and cut altogether in the intervening years and is held up as a symbol of wasteful spending every time a new transportation budget is debated by Congress.

51 By 2007, the total federal investment in walking and bicycling infrastructure had grown to $4.5 billion overall. Advocates saw reaching the 2% mark of federal transportation funding as a major victory. The 1% mark—or $1 per U.S. resident per year spent on cycling and walking projects— was reached in 2000. For perspective, the federal transportation budget is itself less than 2% of the total U.S. budget. See: Gotschi and Mills, "Active Transportation for America: The Case for Increased Federal Investment in Bicycling and Walking," 2008. This paper is a thorough overview of the economics of bicycling and I am indebted to its authors for their framing and research.

52 Figures courtesy of Transportation Alternatives.

53 T. Snyder, "Federal Funding Means More Bike Commuting." *Streetsblog DC*, July 12, 2013.

54 S. Zavestoski and J. Agyeman, eds., *Incomplete Streets*, Routledge, 2014.

55 S. Goodyear, "This Bike Path Also Helps Prevent Flooded Sewers," *The Atlantic Cities*, June 12, 2013. Water and transportation departments often have mutual goals when it comes to creating "green streets" or "greenways." Streets that reduce sewer runoff are increasingly being seen as a necessary investment; and encouraging bicycling on those streets decreases the hazards of toxic runoff from car emissions and brake linings.

56 Personal communication, along with: M. McKisson, "Bicycling Leads to Radical Lifestyle Change," *Inside Tucson Business*, November 12, 2010; M. McKisson, "Cutting the Cord: Why We Are Going Car Light," *Tucson Velo*, March 2, 2011.

57 From the Pima County report on The Loop Path.

58 Millman Medical Index, 2013.

59 "Stress in America Findings," American Psychological Association, November 9, 2010. One in five Americans rate their health as only poor or fair.

60 E. Wilmot, "Sitting for protracted periods increases risk of diabetes, heart disease, death," *Diabetologia*, 2012.

61 J. de Hartog, "Do the Health Benefits of Cycling Outweigh the Risks?" *Environmental Health Perspectives*, 2010.

62 J. Lopez-Zetina, "The link between obesity and the built environment," *Health and Place*, 2006.

63 B. Saelens, et al., "Obesogenic Neighborhood Environments, Child and Parent Obesity," *American Journal of Preventive Medicine*, 2012.

64 S. Goodyear, "Fat City: The Way Your Neighborhood is Built Could be Killing You," *Grist*, May 19, 2011.

65 Smiley, et al., "More Inclusive Parks Planning: Park Quality and Preferences for Park Access and Amenities," *Environmental Justice*, 9:1, 2016. For example, this study that looked at parks access noted that overall minorities do not have lesser walkability, but do have greater social barriers by many metrics.

66 L. Rochon, "Unhealthy Neighborhoods Play a Big Role in Obesity, Diabetes Epidemic," *The Globe and Mail*, May 16, 2011.

67 CDC, 2011.

68 About 3% of the federal budget goes to transportation, with much of this being allocated to aviation and ports.

69 D. Quick, "Bridge pedestrian lane raises activity levels, study reports," *Post and Courier*, May 12, 2008.

70 T. Gotschi, "Costs and Benefits of Bicycling Investments in Portland, Oregon," *Journal of Physical Activity and Health*, 2011. See also: F. Montes, et al., "Do health benefits outweigh the costs of mass recreational programs? An economic analysis of four Ciclovia programs," *Journal of Urban Health*, 2011.

71 J. L. Deffenbacher, L. B. Filetti, T. L. Richards, R. S. Lynch, & E. R. Oetting, "Characteristics of two groups of angry drivers," *Journal of Counseling Psychology*, 2003. For instance, it's been suggested that excessive road rage be treated as a psychological syndrome.

72 "Stress in America Findings," American Psychological Association, November 9, 2010.

73 Nobel-laureate economist Daniel Kahneman did a survey of Texas women about daily activities they enjoyed. Sex and socializing were ranked the highest, while commuting ranked the lowest. See: A. Lowrey, "Your Commute is Killing You," *Slate*, May, 2011. There is evidence to suggest that quite a bit of work stress is related to the commute as well. See: A. Stutzer and S. Frey, "Stress that Doesn't Pay: The Commuting Paradox," *Scandinavian Journal of Economics*, 2008. We find our commutes so stressful that one economic study found we would need a 40% pay increase to make an extra hour of commuting feel worthwhile.

74 R. Martin, "Long Commutes 'Bad for Marriage': Swedish Study," *The Local*, May 24, 2011.

75 Data courtesy of the CDC's Depression Survey. There's a good deal of variation. Northern states, from Montana to Wisconsin have much lower rates, with one in 20 adults being depressed. But one in six adults are depressed in some southern states, notably between Oklahoma and Alabama.

76 E. Jaffe, "The Unsettling Link Between Sprawl and Suicide," *The Atlantic Cities*, July 15, 2013.

77 "People who live by busy roads have 75% fewer friends than those on quiet streets," *Daily Mail*, September 19, 2008.

78 T. Litman, "Valuing Transit Service Quality Improvements," VTPI, 2011.

79 O. Smith, "Commute Well Being Among Bicycle, Car, and Transit Commuters in Portland, Oregon," Dissertation at Portland State University, February, 2013.

80 Darren Buck, "Bikeshare Equity Framework," bikepedantic.wordpress.com, November 29, 2012.

81 M. DeBonis, "Capital Bikeshare possibly underpaid workers, ex-employee alleges," *Washington Post*, May 6, 2013.

82 M. Chaban, "New Leader Will Drive Expansion of CitiBike," *New York Times*, October 28, 2014.

83 C. Szczepanski, "Women's (Bike) History: Kittie Knox," www.blog.bikeleague.org, March 8, 2013; Lorenz J. Finison, *Boston's Cycling Craze, 1880-1900: A Story of Race, Sport, and Society*, U. of Massachusetts Press, May 2014.

84 A. Lugo and N. Doerner, United Spokes: Together in American Streets, Leagues of American Bicyclists, March 2014.

85 Bicycling is high on the list of the book *Stuff White People Like*, which lists obsessions perhaps better categorized as of interest to a politically liberal young person.

86 W. Moritz, "Survey of North American bicycle commuters: Design and aggregate results," *Transportation Research Record: Journal of the Transportation Research Board*, 1578, 91–101, 1997. A 1997 survey of bicycle commuters throughout North America found that the average respondent was a 39 year old man, earning over $45,000. Also see: The Lifestyle Market Analyst, SRDS, 2005. In 2005, a different survey by a marketing company found that cyclists who ride frequently, whether for transportation, sport, or recreation, had a median income of nearly $60,000. Also see:

E. de Place, "Who Bikes?" *Sightline Daily*, April 4, 2011. As recently as 2010, more than 80% of commuters who told the census they primarily used their bicycles for transportation identified as white. (The bicycling rates were close to consistent with the share of population for each race, however).

87 H. Nixon and C. Deluca, "Women's Representation on California's Bicycle Advisory Committees," Mineta Transportation Institute, April 2012.

88 A. Schmitt, "Does the Gender Disparity in Engineering Harm U.S. Cycling?" *Streetsblog*, May 17, 2013.

89 http://www.bikeleague.org. This is the same Dr. Lugo who coined the term "Human Infrastructure" used later in this book.

90 Both these interviews can be seen in the 2015 short film "A League of Their Own" by Elly Blue and Joe Biel, part of our *Groundswell* video project at www.pdot.org.

91 You can read a thorough account of the Albina bike lane controversy, as well as other useful stories about racism and bicycle planning in M.L. Hoffman *Bike Lanes Are White Lanes: Bicycle Advocacy and Urban Planning* (University of Nebraska Press) 2016

92 M. Roth, "SF Responds to Bike Injunction With 1,353 Page Enviro Review," *Streetsblog*, November 28, 2008

93 The bulk of the research in this section comes from the American Lung Association's report on disparities in the impact of air pollution at stateoftheair.org, accessed online on July 18, 2013. See also: "Traffic-Related Air Pollution: A Critical Review of the Literature on Emissions, Exposure, and Health Effects," Health Effects Institute, January 1, 2010.

94 V. Van Wijnen, et al., "The exposure of cyclists, car drivers and pedestrians to traffic-related air pollutants," *International Archives of Occupational and Environmental Health*, 1995; M. Chertok, et al., "Comparison of air pollution exposure for five commuting modes in Sydney—car, train, bus, bicycle, and walking," *Health Promotion Journal of Australia*, 2004; J. Rank, et al., "Differences in cyclists and car drivers exposure to air pollution from traffic in the city of Copenhagen," *The Science of the Total Environment*, 2001; O. Hertel, et al., "A proper choice of route significantly reduces air pollution exposure," *Science of the Total Environment*, 2008; S. Kaur, et al., "Exposure visualisation of ultrafine particle counts in a transport microenvironment," *Atmospheric Environment*, 2006; J. Marshall and E. Behrentz, "Vehicle self-pollution intake fraction: Children's exposure to school bus emissions," *Environmental Science and Technology*, 2005.

95 A. Roberts, et al., "'Perinatal air pollutant exposures and autism spectrum disorder in the children of Nurses' Health Study II participants," *Environmental Health Perspectives*, accessed online on June 18, 2013.

96 R. Hotz, "The Hidden Toll of Traffic Jams," *Wall Street Journal*, November 8, 2011.

97 A. Appatova, et al., in M. Pedroso, "Safe Routes to School: Steps to a Greener Future," 2008.

98 T. Litman, "Congestion Costing Critique: Critical Evaluation of the "Urban Mobility Report," VTPI, 2013. Litman suggests that overall traffic-congestion costs are modest, only increasing time and fuel costs nationwide by 2%—a large number overall, but not nearly as large as costs associated with parking, car ownership, crashes, and pollution damage. He finds, moreover, that the standard methodology used for calculating costs of congestion is unscientific and grossly overestimates costs as well as the benefits of roadway expansion. Large cities are special cases, with congestion being a serious problem; but they are also the places where there is the least room to build more roads; and where the effects of new roads are the worst. Also: A. Schmitt, "Traffic Studies Systematically Overstate the Benefits of Road Projects," *Streetsblog*, July 6, 2012. A study in California found that the net benefits of a road expansion project would be cut in half if it caused just 2% of regional residents to move from an urban to a suburban area, thus creating more traffic.

99 C. Williams-Derry, "Increases in greenhouse-gas emissions from highway-widening projects," Sightline Institute, October 2007.

100 From www.fueleconomy.gov, U.S. Department of Energy, accessed July 18, 2013.

101 M. Dijkema, et al., "Air quality effects of an urban highway speed limit reduction," *Atmospheric Environment*, 2008; L. Hickman, "Speed Limits Reduce Deaths, but Can They Also Cause More Pollution?" *Guardian UK*, April 23, 2010.

102 M. Friedman, et al., "Impact of Changes in Transportation and Commuting Behaviors During the 1996 Summer Olympic Games in Atlanta on Air Quality and Childhood Asthma," *Journal of the American Medical Association*, 2001.

103 D. Q. Rich, et al., "Association between changes in air pollution levels during the Beijing Olympics and biomarkers of inflammation and thrombosis in healthy young adults," *Journal of the American Medical Association*, accessed online on May 15, 2012.

104 Research is consistent—we can't build our way out of congestion. Especially see: R. Noland and W. Cowart, "Analysis of Metropolitan Highway Capacity and the growth in vehicle miles of travel," *Transportation*, 2000; T. Dutzik and R. Pregulman, "More Roads, More Traffic: Why Highway Construction Won't Solve Traffic Congestion in Washington," WashPirg Foundation, 2003.

105 H. Yen, "Sprawling Suburbs Growth Falls to Historic Low Amid High Gas Prices," AP, April 5, 2012.

106 This story is gleaned from the valuable histories of the anti-freeway movement recorded at preservenet.com. San Francisco's Central Freeway was also ruined in the Loma Prieta quake. After years of wrangling, part of that was torn down as well.

107 K. Rao, "Seoul, Korea Tears Down an Urban Highway, Life Goes On," *Grist*, April 4, 2011.

108 B. McMullen, "The Relationship Between VMT and Economic Activity," OTREC, accessed online on June 4, 2012.

109 J. Maus, "City to Unveil Four New Bike Corrals Downtown," *BikePortland*, September 10, 2008.

110 Information courtesy of PortlandAfoot.org, accessed online on July 18, 2013. Five existed previously with prior designs, and five were installed in 2008. In 2009, 30 went in. In 2010, only 21 went in. Bike corrals cost the city $2,200 to $3,000 each to install and represent a 400-800% increase in parking capacity. Any business that regularly has 10 or more bikes parked outside can sign up for the program. Also: D. Meisel, "Bike Corrals: Local Business Impacts, Benefits, and Attitudes," PSU School of Urban Studies and Planning, May 2010. A graduate student interviewed businesses on blocks with bike corrals in 2010. 84% of the businesses surveyed strongly agreed that the corrals were a positive contribution to their block and their business. Benefits reported included better visibility of their business from the street, more room and an improved environment for sidewalk seating, and an increase in the number of customers that arrived by bike.

111 L. Frazer, "Paving Paradise: The Peril of Impervious Surfaces," *Environmental Health Perspectives*, 2004

112 "We Are the 25%: Looking at Street Area Percentages and Surface Parking," *Old Urbanist* (oldurbanist.blogspot.com), December 2011. Older cities, built before cars existed, devote much less space to streets. For example the downtown areas New York City is 28% public right of way, Vienna is 23%, Tokyo is 20%, and Fes, Morocco, is 2% (these figures include streets and sidewalks, but not parking). Also: "Density on the Ground: Cities and Building Coverage," *Old Urbanist*, June, 2011.

113 H. Akbari and L. Rose, "Characterizing the Fabric of the Urban Environment: A Case Study of Salt Lake City, Utah," University of California, Berkeley, February 2001. An additional 20-30% of land area throughout the city was covered by the roofs of buildings.

114 A standard parking space is 325 square feet. As recently as 2012, Manhattan apartments under 300 square feet were listed between $200,000 and $625,000, and renting for nearly $2,000 a month. New York has finally caught on to the benefits of charging market rates for street parking; Manhattan's rates have recently gone up to $3.50 an hour, making the option of living in your van in an actual parking space less competitive than it has been in the past.

115 T. Cowen, "Free Parking Comes at a Price," *New York Times*, August 15, 2010. Shoup's now-classic 2011 tome *The High Cost of Free Parking* is the primer on this topic. Shoup estimates that, including construction and land cost, one LA parking spot is worth $31,000 — more than many of the cars that will be parked on it.

116 T. Litman, "Transportation Cost and Benefit Analysis II – Parking Costs," VTPI, 2012. On street parking costs less than garage parking up front but adds up over time—Todd Litman finds the annual direct costs, without externalities such as land value, to average out at $1,341 in the city and about half that in the suburbs, compared to between $2,800 and $4,000 per space per year for structured parking. Moreover, he finds, the cost to cities for maintaining enough parking for all car-owning residents is $4,400 per car, per year. The rule of thumb is to maintain one residential space and two commercial spaces per vehicle. Car owners pay about a quarter of that cost directly; the rest is a subsidy which we all pay indirectly.

117 K. Mieszkowski, "We Paved Paradise," *Salon*, October 1, 2007. In England parking minimums been removed entirely, thanks to bipartisan efforts—conservatives like deregulation, and liberals like the multitude of public benefits. Portland, Oregon removed parking minimums in the 1980s in areas with frequent transit service, with good success (it has very recently reinstituted them after neighbors of a planned new development feared that on-street parking in that area, which is free, would become hard to find).

118 T. Gotschi and K. Mills, "Active Transportation For America," *Rails to Trails Conservancy*, 2008

119 Pucher, Handy, and Dill, "Infrastructure, programs, and policies to increase bicycling: An international review," *Preventive Medicine*, accessed online on September 16, 2009.

120 Lee and March, "Recognising the Economic Role of Bikes: Sharing Parking in Lygon Street, Carlton," *Australian Planner*, 2010.

Findings are per square meter of parking on retail heavy Lygon Street; 99% of parking space was for cars, 1% for bikes.

121 Eva Ligeti, "Bike Lanes, On Street Parking, and Business," Clean Air Partnership. 2009.

122 As of press time in 2016, word of mouth has it that there has yet to be any traffic fatality in any bike-share system in the U.S.—a rumor to be taken with a grain of salt.

123 B. Fried, "The Citi Bike Story No One's Talking About: Only 3 Injuries in 500,000 Rides," *Streetsblog NYC*, July 3, 2013.

124 N. Kazis, "From London to DC, Bike Sharing is Safer Than Riding Your Own Bike," *Streetsblog*, June 16, 2011. Across other bike sharing systems, the same phenomenon has been found—people using the bike-share have a lower crash rate than is recorded for cycling generally.

125 "Motor Vehicle Accident Report," Police Department, City of New York, April 2013. While it's true that New York City's streets are among the most dangerous in the nation, the presence of cyclists has little to do with that. Far more yellow cabs are involved in crashes than two-wheeled vehicles of any type. And far and away the most common cause of injury or fatal crashes is reported by police to be "Driver Inattention/Distraction."

126 J. Pucher, et al., "Bicycling renaissance in North America? An update and re-appraisal of cycling trends and policies," Transportation Research A, 2011. The number of bicycle trips more than doubled between 2001 and 2009. They went from 1.7 billion in 2001 to 4 billion in 2009. U.S. Department of Transportation and Federal Highway Administration, 2009 National Household Travel Survey Between 1998 and 2008, cycling fatalities didn't go up—they fell by 21%.

127 P. Jacobsen, "Safety in numbers: more walkers and bicyclists, safer walking and bicycling," *Injury Prevention*, 2003.

128 L. Chen, et al., "Evaluating the safety effects of bicycle lanes in New York City, American Journal of Public Health," November 17, 2011. Some more examples of the Safety in Numbers in effect can be found in the Bikes Belong statistics database, including: The installation of many miles of new bike lanes in New York City did not lead to an increase in bike crashes, despite the increase in the number of cyclists. Also see: MCBC Weekly Bulletin for April 3, 2008, Marin County Bicycle Coalition, 2008. In Marin County, CA, bike commuting increased 66% while bicycle crashes declined 34% from 1998 to 2008. Also see: City of Portland Fatality Summary 2007-2008, City of Portland Office of Transportation, 2008; Portland Bicycle Counts 2008. Between 2007 and 2008, overall bicycle use in Portland, Oregon increased 28%. In Portland, OR, 2008 total traffic fatalities were the lowest in recorded history, with only 20 total fatalities, none of them cyclists. In 2008, car, pedestrian, and cyclist fatalities were all at all-time lows. Also see: R. Geffen, "Cheap PR stunt demonises cyclists," European Cyclists' Federation, 2009. In London there has been a 91% increase in bicycling on the capital's main roads since 2000, and a 33% reduction in bicyclist casualties in roughly the same period. Also see: J. Pucher, et al., "Infrastructure, programs and policies to increase bicycling: An international review," Active Living Research Program of the Robert Wood Johnson Foundation, 2009 (tentatively scheduled for publication in *Preventive Medicine*, Feb. 2010). From 1995 to 2003, the number of bicycle trips in Copenhagen made by adults 40 and older rose from 25% to 38%, yet there was a 60% decline in serious injuries. Also see: R. Buehler and J. Pucher, "Cycling to Sustainability in Amsterdam," *Sustain, A Journal of Environmental and Sustainability Issues*, Issue 21, Fall/Winter 2010. Even though 85% of Amsterdam residents ride a bike at least once a week, only six or seven cyclists are killed in traffic accidents every year.

129 More analysis from PeopleForBikes (formerly Bikes Belong): W. Marshall and N. Garrick, "Evidence on Why Bike-Friendly Cities Are Safer for All Road Users," *Environmental Practice* 13, 2011; D. Flusche, "Ridership up, crashes down: 'Safety in Numbers' in Minneapolis," BikeLeague. org blog, February 9, 2011. From 2000 to 2009, bike crashes in Minneapolis, MN dropped 20%, while the number of city bicyclists increased 174% between 2003 and 2008. Also: "NYC DOT Announces Commuter Biking has Doubled in the Last Four Years . . . ," New York City Department of Transportation, 2011. Bicycling in New York City increased 8% between 2010 and 2011, 102% since 2007, and 289% compared to 2001. During the same time, safety increased for all road users.

130 I. Sener, et al., "An Analysis of Bicyclists and Bicycling Characteristics: Who, Why, and How Much are they Bicycling?" 2008. Also see: K. Parker, et al., "If You Build It, Will They Come? The Health Impact of Constructing New Bike Lanes in New Orleans, Louisiana," Presentation Abstract from Active Living Research Conference, 2010.

131 K. Teshke, et al., "Route infrastructure and the risk of injuries to bicyclists: a case-crossover study." *American Journal of Public Health*, 2012. Some types of infrastructure that people do not like to ride do not have that many crashes. This is possibly because the majority of people willing to actually bicycle on them are extremely skilled and confident. But more to the point, busy streets with no bike infrastructure are analogous to bicycle helmets—if they are the only option, then fewer people ride and everyone's safety is reduced. By the same token, multi-use paths, which are the only places many beginning cyclists are willing to ride, see far more crashes than most people are aware, but they also bring out far more users.

132 W. Moritz, "Survey of North American Bicycle Commuters: Design and Aggregate Results," *Transportation Research Record: Journal of the Transportation Research Board*, 1997.

133 Here's plenty more data from PeopleForBikes (formerly Bikes Belong) in support of protected or separated bike lanes, both encouraging more cycling and reducing crashes: R. Noland, "Perceived Risk and Modal Choice: Risk compensation in transportation systems," *Accident Analysis & Prevention*, 27, 503-521, 1995. Bicycle safety improvements attract proportionately more people to bicycling than automobile safety improvements (i.e. a 10% increase in safety results in a greater than 10% increase in the share of people bicycle commuting). Also: C. Reynolds, et al., "The impact of transportation infrastructure on bicycling injuries and crashes: a review of the literature," *Environmental Health* 8:47, 2009. A review of 23 studies on bicycling injuries found that bike facilities (e.g. off-road paths, on-road marked bike lanes, and on-road bike routes) are where bicyclists are safest. Also: "Hennepin and 1st avenues two-way conversion leads to fewer crashes, better access," City of Minneapolis, 2010. After two streets in Minneapolis were converted to be more bicycle friendly, bike traffic increased 43%, total vehicle crashes decreased, traffic efficiency was maintained, and parking revenues remained consistent. Also: H. Wolfson, "Memorandum on Bike Lanes, City of New York," Office of the Mayor, March 21, 2011. When protected bike lanes are installed in New York City, injury crashes for all road users (drivers, pedestrians, and cyclists) typically drop by 40% and by more than 50% in some locations. Also: K. Teschke, et. al., "Route Infrastructure and the Risk of Injuries to Bicyclists: A Case-Crossover Study," *American Journal of Public Health*, 2012. After New York City installed a protected green bike lane on Columbus Avenue, bicycling increased 56% on weekdays Crashes decreased 34% Speeding decreased, Sidewalk riding decreased, traffic flow remained similar, commercial loading hours/space increased 475%. New York City Department of Transportation, 2011 Columbus Avenue parking-protected bicycle path preliminary assessment. A study of 690 bicycling injuries in Canada showed that cycle tracks had the lowest risks.

134 Zayas, Alexandra and Kameel Stanley, "How Riding Your Bike Can Land You in Trouble with the Cops—If You're Black" Tampa Bay Times, April 17, 2015.

134B G. Price, *The Six Percent*, (pricetags.wordpress.com), July 10, 2013.

135 "Causes of Bike Accidents in Long Beach—10 years worth of data," bikelongbeach.org, December 6, 2012.

136 R. Thompson, et al., "A Case-Control Study of the Effectiveness of Bicycle Safety Helmets," *New England Journal of Medicine*, 1989. This paper from Seattle in 1989 found that helmet use reduced head trauma by 85% to 88% among cyclists who had been in a crash. This study is quoted ubiquitously, but it is often misread to mean that the occurrence of head trauma was reduced by almost 90%; what the researchers actually found was that helmets reduced the severity of the injury as much as 88% of the time rather than eliminating it altogether. Moreover, the results of that study hasn't been replicated since—an important step in any scientific finding—and other studies, including a follow several years later by the same team have not been as compelling. What is worse is that the standards for certifying helmet safety are old, dating back decades to a time before the function of the brain was fully understood. Helmet manufacturers and researchers are working to update their knowledge and technology, but it's a long process. In the meantime, there is some research (though again, nothing at all conclusive or replicable—and in these cases not scientifically rigorous) that suggests that wearing a helmet may increase risky cycling behavior and that drivers may not give cyclists in helmets as much passing room as those without. A reporter spent a year investigating the bicycle helmet question for *Bicycling Magazine*, www.bicycling.com/senseless/

137 K. Teschke, et al., "Bicycling: Health Risk or Benefit?" UBCMJ, March 2012.

138 J. Maus, "94% of Bikes Wait at Red Lights, Study Finds," June 25, 2013. A study in Chicago found that after new bicycle signals were put in on the busy downtown Dearborn Avenue, cyclist compliance at red lights nearly tripled, from 31% to 81%. A host of studies have attempted to determine who is at fault more often in crashes involving a car and a bicycle; they universally have found that in at least half the cases and often closer to 90% the driver is to blame. As in Manhattan, we are finding that cities with adequate bicycle infrastructure—and with more people cycling—obey traffic laws at much higher rates than in cities where cyclists must fend entirely for themselves in a hostile environment. New research in Oregon found 94% of people on bicycles stop at red lights. Other cities anecdotally do not boast such law-abiding behavior—but that may be a function in many ways of infrastructure. Research in Chicago found that after new bicycle signals were put in on the busy downtown Dearborn Avenue, cyclist compliance at red lights nearly tripled, from 31% to 81%. A host of studies have attempted to determine who is at fault more often in crashes involving a car and a bicycle; they universally have found that in at least half the cases and often closer to 90% the driver is to blame.

139 A. Goldmark, "Traffic Fatalities Up in NYC, Speeding Top Culprit, DOT Says," WNYC, March 18, 2013.

140 http://www.cdc.gov/injury/wisqars/leadingcauses.html. Until 2009, it was the leading cause of death for those under 35; the reduction in driving that began that year resulting unintentional poisoning to rise to the top for ages 25–64.

141 T. Litman, "Integrating public health objectives in transportation decision-making," *The Science of Health Promotion*, 18, 103–8, 2003.

142 A. Schmitt, "Study: Low income neighborhoods much more likely to have dangerous roads," *Streetsblog DC*, April 24, 2012. Low-income neighborhoods have more dangerous roads, greatest risk of a crash due to roadway design. Much of this is due to traffic volume (a predictor of crashes)—low income neighborhoods were found to have 2.4 times the traffic of high income neighborhoods. Also see: Duncan, et al., "Space, Race, and Poverty: Spatial Inequalities in Walkable Neighborhood Amenities," *Spacial Demography*, Volume 26, May 2012. These dangers have in at least one study (in Boston) been associated with racial segregation in residential neighborhoods.

143 D. Redelmeier and B. McClellan, "Modern Medicine is Neglecting Road Traffic Crashes," *PLoS Medicine*, 2013. A group of global scientists called for this epidemic to be taken seriously in this 2013 paper. They wrote that as of the most recent numbers available, annual losses to traffic crashes amounted to 1.2 million deaths, 20 million survivors with disabilities, and 100 million people with significant economic losses related to property damage.

144 http://www-nrd.nhtsa.dot.gov/Pubs/811741.pdf (the injury data is from the NHTSA's 2011 data). The fatality count is an early estimate for 2012, showing an increase in almost 2,000 fatalities from the previous year.

145 From NHTSA.gov (that's 9% of non-fatal car crashes).

146 "CDC Study Finds Annual Cost of Motor Vehicle Crashes Exceeds $99 Million," CDC Newsroom, August 25, 2010.

147 "Crashes vs Congestion: What's the Cost to Society?" AAA, November 2011.

148 A. Caplan, "Elderly Drivers and Fatal Accidents: Is the Doctor Responsible?" September 12, 2010.

149 Information furnished by Safe Routes to School, http://www.srts.org.

150 D. Livingston, "With no ride to school, African American and Poor Children Disproportionately Hit in Traffic in Urban Districts," *Akron Beacon Register*, June 8, 2013.

151 T. Snyder, "Mom threatened with arrest for letting daughter bike to school," *Streetsblog DC*, September 1, 2011. Theresa Tryon, a mom in Tennessee, was taken to task by police for allowing her daughter to bike to school.

152 J. Duke, et al., "Physical activity levels among children aged 9-13 years: United States, 2002," *Morbidity and Mortality Weekly Report*, 2003.

153 Youth and Obesity Factsheet, http://www.CDC.org.

154 S. Goodyear, "Where you Live Could Make Your Kids Fat," *The Atlantic Cities*, April 2012. Kids who walk and bike to school are 59% less likely to be obese.

155 S. Goodyear, "Kids Who Walk or Bike to School Concentrate Better, Study Shows," *The Atlantic Cities*, February 5, 2013. This Danish study found that exercise had greater impact than diet did on academic performance. Also see: D. Martinez-Gomez, et al., "Active commuting to school and positive cognitive performance in adolescents: The AVENA study," *Archives of Pediatrics and Adolescent Medicine*, 2010.

156 B. Landsberg, et al., "Associations between active commuting to school, fat mass, and lifestyle factors in adolescents: the Kiel Obesity Prevention Study (KOPS)," *European Journal of Clinical Nutrition*, 62, 739–47, 2008.

157 S. Goodyear, "Kids who get driven everywhere don't know where they're going," *The Atlantic Cities*, May, 2012.

158 P. Norton, *Fighting Traffic*, 2008. It's also worth noting that in the Netherlands in the 1970s, that country was entering a similar stage that the U.S. is today, of seriously attempting to improve transportation choices by creating bikeable streets. "Stop the Child Murders" was the rallying cry of the movement against the dominance of the car.

159 C. MacGregor, et al., "Identifying Gaps in Child Pedestrian Safety," *Transportation Research Record*, No. 99-0742.

160 The first edition of this book misstated the mechanism by which teenagers tend to take more risks than adults over 25. For more nuanced reading on this topic, see: B. J. Casey and K. Caudle, "The Teenage Brain: Self Control," *Current Directions in Psychological Science*, 22(2) 82–87, 2013.

161 "Teen Drivers Factsheet," http://www.CDC.gov.

162 More Magnolia Street facts and figures: The 2008 "road diet" including re-striping and signage, added up to $24,000. The Magnolia Green Public Parking Garage was completed in 2006. It provides 320 car parking spaces at the total cost of $5,332,900—or $16,665 per space. Eighty bike parking staples—with a total capacity of 160 bikes—were installed at the total cost of $12,480.42, including racks, shipping, and installation on every block in front of local retail businesses. That breaks down to $156 per rack, or $78 per bicycle parking space.

163 M. Iacono, et al., "Access to destinations: How close is close enough?" Report #4 in the Access to Destination Study, Minnesota Department of Transportation, 2008.

164 In July, 2013, the average gas mileage of new cars on the market is nearly 25 miles per gallon. On average, someone my age drives 15,000 miles in a year. At at these rates, I would be in the market for 600 gallons of gas this year, at a total price of nearly $2,400 for the year, or $200 per month. This hypothetical number holds up to actual spending habits. According to the U.S. Energy Information Administration, Americans spent 4% of our mean household income in 2012, or $2,912 on gas—a higher rate than in previous years even though the amount of driving we did declined.

165 "Where Your Gas Money Goes," *Union of Concerned Scientists*, January, 2013. Of course, part of the cost of driving goes back into the local economy—but not as much as you'd think. If you spend $50 filling up on gas, $33 of that goes straight to the oil company, producing great profits but a limited trickle of overall returns. The oil industry produces a lot of jobs in a few places, but very few compared to the amount of money that changes hands—only one job is created per $1 million of output. By comparison, the retail sector employs 12 people per million dollars of output.

166 Information furnished by the 3/50 Project.

167 J. Cortwright, "Portland's Green Dividend," July 2007. The total savings would be greater today—his analysis was done when gas was still $3 a gallon. He also calculates the value of time that is not spent driving, and it comes out to $1.5 billion, for a total savings each year of $2.6 billion. He adds that this is a sign of prosperity rather than depression; 65% of Portlanders are happy with their transportation system, compared with 30% nationally. And Portland's economy is not worse off than other cities where people drive far more.

168 E. Drennen, "Economic Effects of Traffic Calming on Urban Small Businesses," Department of Public Administration, San Francisco State University, 2003.

169 C. McCormick, "York Blvd: Economics of a Road Diet," 2012. A road diet on York Boulevard in LA removed car lanes, added bike lanes, and did not cause a lack of business.

170 W. Reisman, "Revised options for Polk Street that exclude bike lanes gain support from merchants," *SF Examiner*, April 29, 2013.

171 Information from http://www.bikelongbeach.org: A study after its second year found the by now humdrum results that traffic safety improved immensely and new businesses moved into vacant storefronts citing the increased biking and walking traffic.

172 C. Szczepanski, "How Bicycles Bring Business," *Momentum Magazine*, April 29, 2013.

173 Data from the OHSU Bike Program 2011 Report.

174 "Cycling industry gives economy 3 billion pound boost," BBC, August 22, 2011. The report authors projected that if the UK reaches its goal of raising the bike commute mode share by 20% in the next decade, the savings to the economy could amount to 2 billion pounds a year.

175 B. Fried, "A Bike Company Offers a Prescription for America's Health Care Cost Crisis," *Streetsblog*, March 23, 2012.

176 P. Jensen, et al., "Characterizing the speed and paths of shared bicycles in Lyon," 2010. Getting around many crowded urban areas by bicycling actually is faster (especially if you factor in parking). Lyon, France is a city with no bike lanes, but many bicycles. In 2005 the city launched Velo'v, the first modern bike-share system and the one upon which the contemporary systems sweeping the United States are based. Data captured by the bike-share program and released in 2010 found that bicycle speed over the course of a trip, including stops, averaged 10kmph or 6mph under normal conditions; the same average speed at which you can drive a car around narrow European inner city streets. During rush hour, however, average bike speeds went up to 9mph. Perhaps this is because it is easier to ride a bicycle quickly past cars that are not moving, rather than needing to slow down to dodge quicker vehicles.

177 A bicycle tax credit was passed in the last decade, but it is confusing and rarely used.

178 C. Martin, "In Cargo Delivery, the Three Wheelers that Could," *New York Times*, July 7, 2013.

179 M. Andersen, "Are 'bikes vs trucks' battles fading? Advocates say so," *BikePortland*, June 26, 2013. In fact, advocates for the two interests are beginning to recognize this commonality—two advocates in Oregon recently worked together to alter the design of a street being given a road diet treatment so that users on bicycles and people making freight deliveries would not come into conflict.

180 They chronicle their adventures and share their work at http://www.pathlesspedaled.com

181 K. Clifton, "Business Cycles: Catering to the Bicycling Market," OTREC, 2012.

182 "Economic and Health Benefits of Bicycling," Iowa Bicycle Coalition, January 2012.

183 H. Beierle, "Bicycle Tourism as a Rural Economic Development Vehicle," Department of Planning, Public Policy & Management, U. of Oregon, June 2011.

184 *Outdoor Recreation Report 2013*, Outdoor Foundation, 2013.

185 Information from: http://www.redbikeandgreen.org; I. Hopkins, "Red, Bike, & Green wants to shift the color balance in cycling," *Grist*, 2013; C. Morse, "Red Bike and Green: The Interview!" Project Oakland, May 29, 2012.

186 J. Hobson, "Group tries to increase access to bicycles among African Americans," WBUR: Here and Now, July 5, 2013.

187 H. Sani, "Fighting for Bike Lanes in Atlanta's Historic Black Neighborhood,"http://www.blog. bikeleague.org, November, 2012.

188 "The New Majority: Pedaling Towards Equity," The League of American Bicyclist's report, 2013. This report relies on existing studies and on new market research. People of color is identified in the report as any identification by respondents for race other

than "white." Again, the ridership stats are just for commuters whose primary mode is the bike.

189 A. Leung and A. Mannos, "Bicycling is for Everyone: The Connections Between Cycling in Developing Countries and Low-Income Cyclists of Color in the U.S." *Streetsblog LA*, June 1, 2011.

190 Information from: http://www.ovarianpsycos.com; K. Fortin, "The Ovarian Psycos Bicycle Brigade make a space for women on the eastside," *Streetsblog LA*, March 15, 2012.

191 Information from: U.S. Current Population Survey and the National Committee on Pay Equity; Bureau of Labor Statistics: Weekly and Hourly Earnings Data from the Current Population Survey, accessed at http://www.infoplease.org. A correlation between race and class is problematic in terms of identity and individual cases, but it is a statistical reality in the United States. Perhaps the best example is the income gap. In 2010, white women earned 80 cents on the dollar for the same type of work done by a white man; for that same dollar, Black men earn 75 cents, Black women earn 70 cents, Hispanic men earn 66 cents, and Hispanic women earn 60 cents. This racial component of this gap has not always been so wide, at least among men, but has become more unequal in the recent recession.

192 D. Royal and D. Miller-Steiger, "National Survey of Bicyclist and Pedestrian Attitudes and Behavior," National Highway Traffic Safety Administration, 2008.

193 K. Parker, et al., "Effect of Bike Lane Infrastructure Improvements on Ridership in One New Orleans Neighborhood," *Annals of Behavioral Medicine*, online, January 19, 2013. Incidentally, the cost of adding the bike lane was less than 1% of the budget for repaving the road.

194 Personal communications, and J. Maus, "With six kids and no car, this mom does it all by bike," *BikePortland*. June 28, 2012.

195 The National Household Travel Survey (NHTS) found that bicycle trips to work increased 25% between 2001 and 2009 in the U.S. as a whole; in many cities that increase is much higher. But within these statistics lies a growing gender gap. A 2011 paper by noted bicycle transportation researcher John Pucher pointed out that between 2001 and 2009, the percent of all bicycle trips that were made by women fell from one third to just under one quarter. But the percentage bicycling figured into the overall rate of trips women made remained steady over that period of time at 0.5%. This means that uptick in bicycling numbers nationwide consists mostly of men.

196 U.S. Bureau of Labor Statistics.

197 J. Garrard, S. Handy, and J. Dill, "Women and Cycling," in J. Pucher and R. Buehler, eds., *City Cycling*, MIT Press, 2012.

198 J. Pucher and R. Buehler, "Cycling for everyone: Lessons from Europe," *Transportation Research Record: Journal of the Transportation Research Board*, 2008.

199 A. Broache, "Perspectives on Seattle Women's Decisions to Bike for Transportation," Master's thesis, U. of Washington, 2012.

200 Gluskin Townley Group, American Bicyclist Survey, 2012.

201 D. Royal and D. Miller-Steiger, "National Survey of Bicyclist and Pedestrian Attitudes and Behavior," National Highway Traffic Safety Administration, 2008.

202 A. E. Lugo, "How Critical Mass Built the L.A. Bike Movement," in Carlsson, et al., eds., *Shift Happens: Critical Mass at 20*, (Full Enjoyment) 2012. Lugo's observations on this history can be read in more depth in this essay.

203 I'm indebted to Tom Fucoloro of Seattle Bike Blog for his reporting on sharrows, and for a long walking tour in 2011 that brought many of these points home.

204 In Santa Monica, California, sharrows are used to clarify complicated lane changes at intersections where buses, cars, and bikes are all merging and turning. In Portland, Oregon, they are used solely on residential streets where they serve as way finding signs and also indicate where people should ride—right in the middle of the road, well clear of opening car doors.

205 For more background about the fascinating history of the grassroots anti-car activism of the Netherlands, see: Z. Furness, *One Less Car: Bicylcing and the Politics of Automobility*, Temple University Press, 2010.

206 While Forester does not approve of sharrows, he believes them to be "better than stripes."

207 I am relying here on the thorough reporting of Streetsblog on the saga of Prospect Park West in 2010 through 2012.

208 B. Fried, "Results of the New PPW: Speeding Down Dramatically, Cycling Up Big," *Streetsblog*, October 22, 2010. Before the Prospect Park West bike lane was installed, 3 out of 4 cars exceeded the street's speed limit; afterward only one out of seven were found to be speeding.

209 R. Florida, "America's Top Cities for Bike Commuting: Happier, Too," *The Atlantic*, June 22, 2011. Bicycle-friendly metro areas also rank high for fitness, wealth, and education.

210 Prospect Park West: Traffic Calming & Bicycle Path, NYC DOT, 2012.

211 The details of this connection were reported first on the Daily Kos blog on May 26, 2013.

212 R. Read, "Opponents force Imperial Oil to send megaloads to Canada's oil sands on interstates, avoiding scenic highways," *The Oregonian*, November 7, 2011. Some of the trucks intended to be brought onto scenic highways are 3 stories high and as long as a football field.

213 U.S. Energy Information Administration, 2012.

214 "Road Transportation Emerges as Key Driver of Warming," NASA GISS, February 18, 2010.

215 Numbers provided by http://www.350.org.

216 Also according to 350.org, scientists say that we have about 575 gigatons left to go before temperatures rise to the point that permanently breaks the ecological systems that keep U.S. breathing and above water—but our known oil reserves contain the potential for 2,795 gigatons of carbon emissions.

SUBSCRIBE TO EVERYTHING WE PUBLISH!

Do you love what Microcosm publishes?

Do you want us to publish more great stuff?

Would you like to receive each new title as it's published?

Subscribe as a BFF to our new titles and we'll mail them all to you as they are released!

$10-30/mo, pay what you can afford. Include your t-shirt size and month/date of birthday for a possible surprise! Subscription begins the month after it is purchased.

microcosmpublishing.com/bff

...AND HELP US GROW YOUR SMALL WORLD!

More about bicycle culture and transportation: